'*Green Kitchen Stories* has been a massive inspiration to me over the last few years – it was my go-to blog from the very beginning and I love all their books, too. Everything they create is so beautiful, inventive and delicious – they're a truly unique family and I'm really excited about their new book!'

ELLA WOODWARD, author of *Deliciously Ella*

'The inspired recipes that emerge from David and Luise's kitchen are always fresh, vibrant and truly irresistible. I could happily gaze at their food and photographs all day long.'

AMY CHAPLIN, award-winning cookbook author of *At Home in the Whole Food Kitchen*

'David and Luise have revolutionised our assumptions about "healthy" food – everything they do proves that real food and simple meals can be delicious, gorgeous and decadent.'

CALGARY AVANSINO, author of *Keep It Real* and Contributing Editor, *British Vogue*

'*Green Kitchen Stories* are my total inspiration, creating the perfect marriage of healthy and delicious. Get ready to see healthy as a way of life: this book is a must!'

MADELINE SHAW, author of *Get the Glow*

'*Green Kitchen Smoothies* is packed with vibrant, energizing, and unique smoothie and juice recipes. Every smoothie-lover needs this inspiring cookbook in their repertoire!'

ANGELA LIDDON, *New York Times* bestselling author of the *Oh She Glows* cookbook and founder of *OhSheGlows.com*

GREEN KITCHEN SMOOTHIES

—

HEALTHY AND COLOURFUL SMOOTHIES FOR EVERY DAY

—

David Frenkiel &
Luise Vindahl

hardie grant books

CONTENTS

INTRODUCTION

The first drink Luise and I shared together was *not* a smoothie. Instead it was an absurdly strong Cuba Libre with muddled lime, ice, at least a quarter bottle of dark rum and only a touch of cola in it. It was mixed by my friend at a late-night afterparty in a tiny apartment close to Campo de' Fiori in Rome, Italy. It was probably the very opposite of a smoothie but if it wasn't for that drink, I don't think we ever would have made any smoothies together.

Fast forward nine years and we have since then moved to Stockholm and had two children, Elsa, six, and Isac, one-and-a-half. During this time we also started the food blog *Green Kitchen Stories*, which eventually allowed us to change careers to work full-time with food, nutrition and photography. Luise refuses to give all the credit to that Cuba Libre, but personally, I'm pretty grateful for it.

Today we spend a large part of our days in the kitchen and behind the camera, creating wholesome plant-based recipes for our blog, apps, books, workshops and whatever freelance work we manage to squeeze in. We both love to cook, but with the inevitable recipe fails that are bound to happen when you experiment in the kitchen, long freelance working hours and two kids running laps around our legs, smoothies have become a necessity in our lives. They are a quick, easy

and delicious way to refill energy before the dinner is ready, and also a great way to sneak some extra vegetables into our kids' diet.

We often make smoothies for breakfast, sometimes as a healthier midday alternative to sweet snacks and drinks, other times for dessert and always after a workout. One of our favourite things about smoothies is that they don't call for special kitchen ninja skills like, let's say, making a lemon meringue cake does. The only skill needed is basically just knowing how to chop and push a button. Even Elsa has started making her own smoothies now (with our supervision when she uses the blender).

Since smoothies have become such a common meal for us, we have also picked up some tricks and ideas on how to make them more interesting and varied. Some days call for quick-and-easy smoothies simply poured into a glass. Other days we add extra berries, fruit, nuts or grains unmixed to the glass to create a contrast in flavour and texture. We also tend to pour them in layers for a more interesting and visual drinking experience. Another trick is to make them a little thicker, pour into a bowl, cover with toppings and eat with a spoon. They're delicious and more nourishing as you have a larger area to fit toppings on.

We have gathered all those different types of smoothies in this book. Our hope is that both experienced smoothie enthusiasts and newbies can find new drinks to love. For that reason, we have divided the two main chapters into Simple Smoothies and Showstoppers. Simple Smoothies has all our favourite fast and simple recipes that suit everyone and are easy to shop for, like our ultimate go-to Simple Raspberry Smoothie (page 38) – an easy, great-tasting smoothie made with basic ingredients and no superfoods. Showstoppers are our more intriguing-looking smoothies, like the Peanut Butter & Jam Milkshake (page 68), where the strawberries in the bottom of the glass paint beautiful patterns as you pour over the shake. Impressive as it may look, it takes no more than five minutes to make and has only five ingredients! Needless to say, it also tastes divine. Most of the showstopping smoothies are, in fact, easier than they look.

Apart from the smoothies, we have included a small Basic Recipes chapter with the muesli, granola, nut butter and chia pudding (pages 26–31) that we refer to in many of the other recipes.

There is also a chapter on Juices – the sister of smoothies with more vegetables, less fruit and no fibre. And one chapter with our favourite nut milk blends. Some of them also include a few unusual ingredients like chia seeds, beans, açaí and pumpkin. We finish the book with a Desserts chapter, which includes smoothies that are more on the sweeter side, as well as two frozen varieties.

Over the next couple of pages we will explain how to use this book, list some ingredients that can be good to stock up on, as well as share some helpful tips and tricks to improve your blends. We have also included a quick guide to what tools and appliances you might need.

Most of the recipes in this book are entirely new and previously unpublished. We have included some favourites that we created through years of blogging and also from the smoothie section of our app. All of the smoothies have been tested thoroughly, not only by us but also by a separate tester (thank you, Nic!), and all of the recipes can be made dairy- and gluten-free.

We hope that you will find this book inspiring and helpful. And if you just incorporate a few of these smoothies into your weekly or monthly routine, you will discover how much easier it is to get through long days feeling energized from the inside out.

DAVID

HOW TO USE
THIS BOOK

Blending smoothies isn't a science and shouldn't be; therefore, we have tried to keep the recipe instructions short and easy. We have specified weights when we felt it was needed, but realize that most of you won't weigh your ingredients anyway and have therefore tried to use average-sized fruit and vegetables.

When it comes to flavour, we ask for your help. The sweetness of bananas or creaminess of avocados varies a lot depending on how ripe they are; some dates are half the size of others; and mangos picked ripe and eaten in Mexico or Southeast Asia are a whole different story from the ones that are picked while still green and shipped far away. Adapt the ingredients to what is in season where you live or stock up on frozen fruit and vegetables. And make it a habit to *always* taste the smoothie while still in the blender. Are the flavours balanced? Does it need more sweetness or tartness? We know how we want it to taste, but you are the one drinking it, so trust your own instincts.

As we mentioned in the introduction, we drink smoothies for breakfast, as a midday snack, after a workout or as a dessert. We usually don't replace our main meals with smoothies unless it is a really busy day or we need to give our digestive system and cleansing organs a break.

MEASUREMENTS & CUPS

One average serving is equivalent to about 250 ml (8½ fl oz/1 cup) in this book, unless stated otherwise.

1 cup = 250 ml (8½ fl oz)
½ cup = 125 ml (4 fl oz)
⅓ cup = 80 ml (3 fl oz)
¼ cup = 60 ml (2 fl oz) = 4 tablespoons
1 tablespoon = 3 teaspoons = 15 ml (½ fl oz)
1 teaspoon = 5 ml (¼ fl oz)
1 handful = 30 g (1 oz)

TOO SWEET?

Most smoothies in this book are sweetened with bananas, dates, apples, mango or pineapple – natural and unrefined sweeteners that we love to use. They do, however, still spike the blood sugar, even though less and slower than refined sugar and syrups. Natural sugar from fruit is always a healthier choice than processed, refined and chemically made sugar as the body and brain process it differently.

If you have diabetes or any allergies to bananas or high-fructose fruit, you can still make most of the smoothies in this book with a few substitutions. Banana or mango can easily be swapped for avocado as it adds the same creaminess and yield without being sweet. Apples or pineapple can be replaced with cucumber. And dates can be left out entirely, or you can use a lesser amount. Stevia or Xylitol are natural sweeteners that are known to keep blood sugar levels balanced while still adding sweetness, so try combining it with avocado for a sweet flavour and creamy texture. Make sure to choose good quality products from the health food store. Berries have beautiful flavours, colours and texture and contain almost no fruit sugar, so they are ideal for making low-sugar smoothies.

SMOOTHIES VS JUICES

There is an ongoing debate about whether juices or smoothies are better for you. We make both smoothies and juices in our home and have therefore included a couple of our favourite juices in this book as well. Smoothies and juices have different health aspects and it's impossible to say that one ultimately is better than the other. What suits you best depends on your goals and current state of health. We believe in a combination of the two and that is probably what is best for most people.

SMOOTHIES pulverize all the ingredients and therefore all of the fibre from the produce is included. However, the blending process breaks the fibres apart, making them easier to digest than when eaten raw. Fibre is good for you – it is food for the healthy bacteria in your digestive tract. Fibre also slows down the absorption of sugar and at the same time the absorption of nutrients (the opposite of juices). Smoothies also slow down the digestion and keep you full longer. They oxidize slower than juices and maintain the majority of the nutrients for a longer amount of time.

JUICES extract the liquid from the fruit and vegetables and discard the indigestible/insoluble fibres, making nutrients highly concentrated and more easily absorbed into the bloodstream. Juices also give the digestive system a pause, as your body doesn't have to break down the food before absorbing the nutrients. Juice is not considered a meal replacement because of its lack of protein and fibres but is popular for cleansing. To avoid spiking blood sugar when consuming juices, keep the amounts of fruit low or eliminate it entirely.

OUR SMOOTHIE PANTRY

Here is a short list of the ingredients that we always try to keep in our pantry, fridge and freezer to be able to create smoothies every day. Check out the guide on pages 16–17 to how to combine these (and many more) ingredients into well-balanced smoothies.

FRUIT

BANANAS Bananas are sweet and creamy when blended and therefore ideal in smoothies. They are rich in fibre, magnesium, potassium and vitamin B6. Always use ripe bananas in smoothies, ideally the ones that are just starting to have small brown spots on the skins. You can freeze bananas if they are starting to look too ripe; just follow the method on page 22.

If you are allergic to bananas, replace them with ripe pears, peaches, mango or avocado.

DATES Fresh dates have a very sweet taste and are absolutely delicious in smoothies. They are high in fruit sugar and should be consumed as a treat. We always buy unpitted dark brown dates that are very soft to touch, about 4 cm (1½ in) long and taste of caramel. Medjool dates are great, but often quite expensive. There are, however, many other similar, but less expensive varieties to look for. We buy our dates in paper boxes (40 in each box) that are sold in the fruit section. They are not to be mistaken for the round green, yellow or red fresh dates that are picked before they get wrinkly and often sold still attached to their branches. You should also stay away from dates that are coated in a syrup; they are sweet enough on their own.

If your dates seem very dried and tough, you need to soak them in hot water for at least 15–20 minutes or they will be too hard to blend. Since all varieties of dates are different in size, sweetness and texture, we have left a little leeway with the measurements. The dates we use are quite big so we normally use the lesser amount in the recipes. Always taste your smoothie to see if you think it is sweet enough, and add more dates if needed.

APPLES Apples are loaded with vitamins, minerals, antioxidants and pectin and are one of the healthiest fruits in the world. Crispy, seasonal apples taste like nature's candy and during the Scandinavian autumn and winter, we always keep them at home. Just like berries, apples don't affect blood sugar significantly, making them ideal to sweeten green juices and smoothies. Simply wash and core the apples before juicing or blending them.

MANGO Mango is alkalizing and contains certain enzymes with stomach-comforting properties. It is also high in vitamin A. When mangos are picked ripe they are incredibly sweet and juicy. However, they are often picked while still hard and green to make it through long transportations and they then generally taste a lot less sweet. If your mangos don't taste sweet or juicy enough for your smoothies, you can squeeze some extra orange juice or add half a banana to compensate.

We often keep organic frozen mangos in our freezer and use them if we can't get hold of sweet fresh mangos.

BERRIES When in season, our fridge is absolutely crammed with fresh raspberries, strawberries, lingonberries, blackberries, sea buckthorn and blueberries. They are our favourite fruit to eat and add to smoothies and we just can't get enough. During the rest of the year, we keep our freezer stocked up with them. We either freeze berries ourselves or buy organic frozen berries in the supermarket. Berries are the fruit lowest in fruit sugar and highest in nutritional value, including antioxidants and other phytonutrients. A true superfood!

In some countries, it is recommended to pour boiling water over frozen berries and leave to sit for one minute to kill any viruses before adding them to smoothies (especially when served to elderly people, pregnant women, sick people or children). We usually don't do that with berries that we have picked ourselves or know the origins of, but always check your local recommendations. And do rinse fresh berries in water.

AVOCADO Ripe avocados are creamy, spreadable and rich with healthy fats. They add a very creamy texture to smoothies and pair well with greens, citrus fruit and tropical fruit. Avocado is an important source of fat that your body needs and is good for cell repair and growth.

LIQUIDS

NUT MILKS The obvious reason for drinking almond milk, cashew milk or hazelnut milk is because they are dairy-free, but they are also great in smoothies as they add a delicious richness to them and are high in healthy fats and protein. They are quite expensive so we tend to make our own, also because most brands in stores are filled with sweeteners, thickeners and additives. Look for plant milks containing purely nuts, seeds or grains, water, sea salt and maybe fortified with vitamin D and calcium. Or make your own from any of the recipes in the Nut Milks chapter (page 106).

OAT MILK Oats are one of our most common grains in Scandinavia and we therefore tend to use oat milk more than other varieties. We recommend adapting our recipes to where you live and your specific needs, so if oat milk is hard to come by, use brown rice milk instead or choose a grain-free alternative, like almond milk. Oat milk has a sweet flavour but is naturally unsweetened, just like most rice milks are. We usually buy our oat milk in stores, since delicious, organic pure oat milk is available everywhere for a reasonable price. It can also be made at home by simply replacing the nuts with whole oat groats in our Basic Nut Milk recipe (page 108).

COCONUT MILK Regardless of its name, coconut is in fact not a nut but a seed, part of the palm family. Therefore, it is usually safe for people with nut-tree allergies. We use coconut milk, coconut drinking milk and coconut water as liquid bases in many of our smoothies and we add cold-pressed coconut oil for extra fat and desiccated coconut and chips for toppings.

COCONUT WATER Coconut water is the liquid that is extracted from fresh coconuts. It has a naturally sweet and slightly tropical flavour and is a natural source of electrolytes, which you lose when you sweat. This makes coconut water a good choice of post-cardio drink to prevent dehydration. Bottled coconut water is always pasteurized to last longer, unless it says raw on the bottle. You can also buy a fresh young coconut and use the liquid inside. Fresh coconut flesh is great for thickening smoothies, but we haven't used it in this book since it can be quite difficult to find in many parts of the world.

YOGHURT We add yoghurt to smoothies for the addition of healthy good bacteria, the fresh flavour and creamy texture. We always use plain unsweetened yoghurt. When we layer yoghurt with smoothie, we often choose Greek or Turkish since they are deliciously creamy and high in fat. Check the label to see if the yoghurt contains live and active cultures, which means that the yoghurt has probiotics. Probiotics are good bacterial strains that benefit your health and are important to keep in your diet regularly. Other sources of probiotics are sauerkraut (or other lacto-fermented vegetables), kimchi, kefir, kombucha, miso, tempeh or probiotic supplement powders (which can be added to smoothies).

NUTS & SEEDS

Nuts and seeds are rich in mighty minerals, vitamins, healthy fats and fibre. And we are addicted to them. We try to always keep an assortment of cashew nuts, almonds, hazelnuts, sunflower seeds, pumpkin seeds, chia seeds, hemp seeds, sesame seeds and flaxseeds in our pantry. Apart from that, we also keep nut butter, tahini (sesame seed butter) and coconut oil there. It's an incredible luxury to simply grab a few nuts and seeds to top our smoothie bowls, add into smoothies, to make nut milk (page 106), to bake nut and seed bread or to make nut butter (page 26). Choose natural nuts and seeds, with no added salt or oils.

VEGETABLES

BEETROOT The purple-coloured vegetable should be on your most-often-eaten-vegetable list. It is extremely healthy. It helps the body to fight inflammations, cleans the liver, enhances performance, builds your blood and helps prevent chronic diseases. It has an earthy and sweet flavour and is delicious paired with berries, other roots or even chocolate!

When we use beetroot in this book, we always refer to raw beetroot, not the cooked and peeled ones that can also be found in supermarkets. Beetroots vary vastly in size and this affects the flavour and texture of smoothies quite a bit, so we have included weight measurements in these recipes.

CARROTS We always, always have carrots in our fridge. They are great to cook with, good in juices and smoothies and both our kids love snacking on them raw as well.

Carrots are not expensive either, which is always a plus. Carrots are good for your skin, hair, immune system and eyes.

SPINACH We usually buy organic baby spinach when we use fresh. But we also always keep frozen spinach in our freezer. Frozen vegetables (and fruit) are actually full of nutrients and are often available. They are usually picked, cleaned and frozen within a very short time span, which means they contain more nutrients than some of the supermarket vegetables that can stay on the shelves for weeks. Spinach is a good source of folic acid, and is rich in iron and plant protein.

KALE AND BROCCOLI (CRUCIFEROUS VEGETABLES) Plants from the brassica family (kale, broccoli, cauliflower, Brussels sprouts, rocket leaves, collard greens, romanesco, bok choy and cabbage) are super-healthy and we try to eat a lot of different kinds throughout the year, and use a majority of them in our smoothies too. They are anti-inflammatory, lower oxidative stress in the cells and have detoxifying properties. Buy them organic, fresh or frozen.

FENNEL This liquorice-tasting vegetable adds a nice twist in flavour to juices, green smoothies or berry smoothies. Choose a creamy white and hard bulb with green top fronds attached (which can also be blended). Fennel is particularly high in vitamin C and potassium, which is important for your overall health. It is also known to aid digestion problems.

GINGER Ginger is a marvellous root with many healthy benefits that you can purchase in almost all supermarkets around the world. It is a key-ingredient when making smoothies and juices as it adds a hot and fresh flavour that balances the sweet fruit and savoury vegetables.

SUPERFOOD POWDERS & PROTEIN POWDERS

Powders are popular add-ins to smoothies as they are basically highly concentrated nutrients that can be absorbed by the body easily. When we have them at home we use them to boost smoothies, sprinkle over food, stir into porridge or add to raw truffles. The super green powders (barley grass, spirulina, wheatgrass, matcha) have an alkalizing effect in the body, which is good for optimal health. The powders made from berries, roots and fruits (maca, lucuma and mesquite) are high in antioxidants and phytonutrients and are good for your hormonal balance.

Protein powders can be useful to ensure optimal protein intake and are good to add to post-workout smoothies. It is important to choose a quality brand made from hemp, brown rice, pumpkin seeds, peas or whey. Talk to a nutritionist in a wholefood store to get a good product that suits your needs.

Good-quality powders are generally very pricey and we have therefore not used them a lot in this book. They are not a necessity, but definitely an easy option to get a concentrated amount of healthy nutrients at once. If you have any powders at home, they can of course be added for an extra boost to any of our recipes. If you are looking to buy superfood powders, it's best to get one green blend and one red blend and alternate them in your smoothies. And perhaps one protein powder for when you are working out.

CREATING A PERFECT SMOOTHIE

There is an endless number of ingredient combinations when making a smoothie, but by following these simple steps you are bound to end up with a nutritious, well-balanced and delicious drink. Always aim to have at least one frozen element in the smoothie to get it perfectly chilled and also creamy – it can be any of the fruits or the vegetables.

1 START WITH YOUR BASE

Water

Coconut water

Milk or plant milk (unsweetened)

Fruit juice (not from concentrate)

Vegetable juice (not from concentrate)

Plain yoghurt (unsweetened)

Kefir

Tea (chilled)

2 CHOOSE YOUR FRUIT

Banana

Berries

Cherries

Mango

Apple

Pineapple

Peach

Pear

Avocado

Persimmon

Papaya

Orange

Grapefruit

Grapes

Kiwi

Passion fruit

Cooked pumpkin

3 CHOOSE YOUR VEG

Spinach

Romaine lettuce

Kale

Chard

Celery

Cucumber

Bell pepper

Broccoli

Rocket leaves

Dandelion greens

Carrots

Fennel

Courgette (zucchini)

4 CHOOSE BOOSTERS & FLAVOURINGS

Dry spices (cinnamon, ginger, cardamom, turmeric, saffron)

Fresh herbs

Fresh ginger

Fresh turmeric

Cacao powder or nibs

Nuts

Desiccated coconut

Seeds

Protein powders (hemp, pea, brown rice, whey)

Superfood powders

Bee pollen

Coffee (chilled)

5 ADD A HEALTHY FAT (OPTIONAL)

Coconut oil

Flax oil

Olive oil

Omega-3 oil from fish or algae

Evening primrose oil

6 MAKE IT THICKER & CREAMIER (OPTIONAL)

Nut butter

Seed butter

Chia seeds

Flaxseeds

Psyllium seeds

Rolled oats (or cooked oatmeal)

Unsweetened Greek yoghurt

Cooked white beans

Tofu (silken or soft)

7 ADD AN EXTRA SWEETENER (OPTIONAL)

Soft dates

Dried figs, prunes or apricots

Raw honey

Pure maple syrup

Stevia

TOOLS & EQUIPMENT

While we are not kitchen gadget experts, we have worked our way through a couple of blenders, juicers and food processors. Here are our five cents on what is important when you are looking to buy new equipment.

BLENDER

A good blender is essential for anyone who wants to get serious with smoothies. What brand and model you need depends on your budget and how often you plan to use it. Consider these things when choosing a blender:

* Will you make more than three smoothies a week?

* Will you use it to crush ice?

* Will you be making nut milk?

* Will you add hard vegetables (beetroot, carrots, etc) to it?

* Will you be using it for more people than yourself?

The more questions you've answered yes to, the more money it is probably worth splurging on a good, high-speed blender.

After having burnt out a few cheaper blenders, we have realized that you often get what you pay for. Every time one of our old blenders died, we wished that we had invested in a better brand earlier. We have

also noticed that when you have a good blender, you start to make smoothies more often. So it's not just an investment for your kitchen, but also in yourself.

We finally saved up to get a Vitamix, which is one of the more expensive, high-end models. It is pretty amazing and we have yet to find an ingredient that it hasn't been able to liquefy. We have also tried the similarly expensive Blendtec and it's excellent as well. Another good thing about these types of high-end blenders is that they give a long-term warranty – between five and ten years is typically the norm.

Of course, you don't have to get one of the exclusive brands. There are tons of cheaper brands available and many are great for all your basic needs. With so many different brands, it's difficult to give any specific guidance, but look for machines with wide jugs (to make it easier for all ingredients to get blended), stainless steel blades and strong motors. If they have a tamper (to help push down any ingredients that get stuck), it's a plus, and it's a good sign if they give a long warranty. Another piece of important advice is to read the customer reviews online.

One popular version of smoothie blenders is the NutriBullet-type. Built to maximize nutrients, it is very compact, serves 1–2 people/portions and costs less. If you have a blender that isn't very strong, you can read our tips on page 23 on how to help the blender make smoother smoothies.

FOOD PROCESSOR

A food processor has a wide, flat bottom and a sweeping blade that can mix without any added liquid. It is ideal for shredding, slicing, mincing, grinding and chopping, and especially when done in a large quantity. It is perfect if you cook regularly for a family and it is also the best tool for making our Nut Butter (page 26). We have a Magimix and it is really strong and not too loud.

Other uses for food processors include mixing biscuit dough, cake batter, raw food desserts, baby food, hummus and other spreads, dressings and salsas. A blender or hand blender can do some of these things as well. A food processor certainly can make a smoothie, but we mainly use our food processor for drier textures (solids), to slice or chop large amounts of veggies and to make nut butters, leaving the blender more for mixing liquids.

HAND (IMMERSION) BLENDER

Using a hand blender to make smoothies is a little trickier, but not impossible. We recommend blending in a tall, wide glass bottle or jar instead of using a wider bowl. Hand blenders are very versatile and easy to clean, but if you are looking to make some of our showstopping smoothies, it will be a lot easier using a proper high-speed blender. In our previous kitchen, the hand blender was our most used gadget as it didn't take up much space and came with a food

processor attachment that made it a great little all-in-one tool. So, perfect if you have a small kitchen.

JUICERS

Our first juicer was a centrifugal. It's a high-speed juicer that crushes the produce against a blade, strains the juice and discards the pulp. The good thing about centrifugal juicers is that they are cheaper. They are also easy to clean and have a wide mouth so you can feed in quite large chunks. They are, however, not very good at juicing green leaves and the high speed oxidizes the juice, leaving fewer nutrients. If you have never juiced before, though, centrifugal juicers are a good stepping-stone to getting hooked. If you to want use leaves in it, we find it easier to roll them into balls first, and then add them together with other ingredients.

Slow juicers, or masticating juicers, are more expensive, but a lot better at keeping nutrients and getting more juice out of leafy greens. Even though they are called slow juicers, time is not an issue. They juice pretty quickly. We use a Hurom juicer and it creates delicious juices with intense flavours. Our juicer also looks better than many of the other brands, which is good because you want to keep it out and therefore remember to use it more often.

TIPS & TRICKS

FROZEN BANANAS

We use frozen bananas in many recipes in this book. They are one of the best things to keep in your freezer if you plan on making a lot of smoothies as they make them deliciously creamy and chilled without the addition of ice. Frozen bananas last for months in the freezer, so it's a very convenient way to always have them on hand. Apart from smoothies, frozen bananas are essential for making 'nice cream' (page 145). We always freeze our bananas when they are quite ripe and brown spots start showing.

METHOD:

1. Peel the bananas and chop them into 1.5 cm (½ in) thick slices. You can chop them thicker, but thinner slices are easier for the blender.

2. Spread out the slices (to prevent the bananas from sticking together as they freeze) on a baking tray or chopping board covered in parchment paper and place in the freezer overnight.

3. When frozen, scoop them into freezer-proof containers or zip-lock bags (one banana per serving, around 10–15 slices) and keep in the freezer until needed.

FROZEN AVOCADOS & MANGOS

We freeze avocados and mangos and use them in the same way as bananas. They also keep in the freezer for months. Wait until they are very soft and ripe to get maximum flavour. You can squeeze a little lime or lemon juice on top of the avocados to keep them from turning brown. Remove the peel and stone and cut into 2.5 cm (1 in) cubes or slices. Then follow steps 2 and 3 from the frozen banana method.

FROZEN LIQUIDS

You can freeze liquids such as fresh orange or apple juices and nut milks. It's a better option than adding ice cubes if you need to chill your smoothie as it doesn't dilute the flavour.

SMOOTHIE PACKS

Pre-made frozen smoothie packs are a simple trick to save time and always have a healthy, fulfilling drink in no time. We usually prepare a couple of smoothie packs at a time. Choose your favourite smoothie, for example Green Goodness Bowl (page 72). Wash and prep the ingredients for one or two servings, except any liquids, then place them in individual zip-lock bags and freeze. When you want to make a smoothie, simply place all the frozen ingredients from a zip-lock bag in a blender and add the suggested liquid from the recipe, blend and you have a smoothie. Depending on the blender, you might need to let the ingredients thaw slightly first.

STORING

To avoid vitamin levels decreasing, always store smoothies and juices in sealed jars. We use glass jars and bottles with an airtight lid. If stored this way, they can keep for up to 48 hours.

THE SMOOTHEST SMOOTHIES

Unless you have a mega-strong blender, it can sometimes be difficult to get a completely smooth consistency. Here are a few tricks to keep in mind:

* When you blend leafy greens, start by blending them just with the liquid until completely smooth. Then add the rest of the ingredients.

* When a recipe calls for harder roots like carrot, beetroot or ginger, you can grate them before adding them to the blender.

* If you make nut milks, soak the nuts until they are fully soft. Use a nut milk bag to filter away the grits and pulp.

* Let frozen berries and vegetables thaw for a bit before blending.

* If your blender is having trouble getting dates completely smooth, try soaking them in hot water for 15–20 minutes to soften them up. Or look for softer dates. Medjool-type dates usually work best.

ORGANIC

Raw fruit and vegetables are the main ingredients in smoothies. Unfortunately, they are often sprayed heavily with pesticides and that's not an ingredient we're recommending in our recipes. Cleaning and rinsing your produce is an important first step, but not always very effective as some pesticides move within the plant tissue (synthetic pesticides in general). We therefore recommend choosing organic produce as much as your budget allows. Since organic produce can be quite expensive, we use the Dirty Dozen and Clean Fifteen lists compiled by the Environmental Working Group (EWG) in the US as a guide to which ingredients are most contaminated and therefore worth buying organic. We have shortened the EWG list to include the ingredients that are most relevant for this book.

DIRTY	CLEAN
Apples	Avocados
Peaches and nectarines	Pineapple
Strawberries	Cabbage
Grapes and raisins	Peas (frozen)
Celery	Kiwi
Spinach	Mangos
Peppers	Sweet potatoes
Cucumbers	Grapefruit
Kale	Cantaloupe melon
Cherry tomatoes	

BASIC RECIPES

—

Before we are ready to bring out the blender, we wanted to share a couple of basic recipes that we refer to in many places throughout the book. It's our method for making creamy nut and seed butters that add richness and take your blends to the next level (page 26). Crunchy granola clusters that we often top our smoothies and bowls with (page 29). Delightful chia puddings that are great little snacks and perfect for making layered parfaits (page 28). And an unsweetened muesli recipe that we add to our breakfast smoothies for extra sustenance and texture (page 31).

All these basic recipes are on regular rotation in our house, but we often change them up a bit depending on what we have at home. We sometimes add dried fruit to our granola, lime zest into our chia pudding or mix a little maple syrup and cinnamon into our nut butter. We recommend that you do the same and make these your own.

NUT BUTTER

MAKES 600 g
1 lb 5 oz/2 cups

Our little family is nuts about nut butter. We spread it on rye bread, stir it through porridge, blend it in smoothies, dollop it on chia puddings and even freeze it in popsicles! We like to make our own nut butter as not only do we know what's in it, it's also a cheaper option. Although some brands do add hydrogenated oils, refined sugar and additives, these ingredients are actually completely unnecessary as all you need is nuts, which are rich in healthy monounsaturated and polyunsaturated fatty acids and energy. Generally we use a combination of nuts and sunflower seeds, as they are more affordable and add flavour, but feel free to make a pure nut butter if you prefer. When toasted and ground in a food processor, the nuts slowly release their natural oils and transform into a smooth butter – it's quite fascinating really!

* We like to use equal amounts of almonds, cashew nuts, brazil nuts and sunflower seeds.

600 g (1 lb 5 oz/4 cups) raw nuts of choice (or a combination of nuts and seeds)*
½ teaspoon sea salt

TIP: If you prefer a crunchier texture, try adding some chopped nuts towards the end of blending in the food processor.

Preheat the oven to 150°C/300°F/Gas mark 2. Spread the nuts out in a single layer on a baking tray and toast for 10–20 minutes or until golden. Remove from the oven and set aside to cool.

Put the nuts and salt in a food processor and blend on a high speed for 10–20 minutes or until completely smooth. Stop and scrape down the sides with a spatula every now and again, which also helps prevent your food processor from overheating.

Pour into a sterilized medium-sized sealable glass jar, cool and store in the fridge.

If sealed, the nut butter can keep for a few weeks in the fridge.

CHIA PUDDING

MAKES 250 ml
8½ fl oz/1 cup

—

NUT-FREE

Chia pudding topped with fresh berries and chopped nuts is a wonderful little treat to have for breakfast, a snack or even dessert. However, in this book we like to pair it with our smoothies to create beautiful layers, like in our Mango & Chia Parfait (page 64) and Kiwi, Kale & Chia Parfait (page 99). If you have a sweet tooth, you can always add a touch of pure maple syrup or raw honey, but if you combine the chia pudding with one of our sweet smoothies, there's no need to add a natural sweetener.

———

3 tablespoons chia seeds of choice
¼ teaspoon vanilla powder or 1 teaspoon vanilla extract
1 tablespoon pure maple syrup or raw honey (optional)
250 ml (8½ fl oz/1 cup) unsweetened plant milk

———

Put the chia seeds, vanilla and maple syrup (if using) in a bowl. Pour over the milk and mix until well combined. Stir every now and again in the first 10 minutes to prevent lumps from forming.

Spoon into a medium-sized sealable glass jar and set aside to soak in the fridge for at least 30 minutes or overnight. It's ready when the chia seeds form a gelatinous substance around themselves and the overall consistency is thick and jelly-like. It can keep for a couple of days in the fridge, if unopened.

TIP: *For the Coconut Chia Pudding featured in the Mango & Chia Parfait and Kiwi, Kale & Chia Parfait, we recommend using white chia seeds, ¼ teaspoon lime zest (instead of a natural sweetener) and coconut drinking milk or tinned coconut milk.*

COCONUT & BUCKWHEAT GRANOLA

MAKES 875 g
2 lb/7 cups
—

What we love about this granola, apart from its 'coconutty' flavour, is the crunchy clusters it forms when baked. This granola is ideal on top of our smoothie bowls, like our Açaí Bowl Extra Everything! (page 82) and Kiwi, Kale & Chia Parfait (page 99), or simply sprinkled on yoghurt. We tend not to make our granola too sweet, but feel free to add an extra dash of maple syrup if you wish.

—

We like to use almonds, pumpkin seeds and sesame seeds.

—

150 g (5 oz/1 cup) mixed raw nuts and seeds*
400 g (14 oz/4 cups) rolled oats (choose certified gluten-free if allergic)
100 g (3½ oz/½ cup) raw buckwheat
80 g (3 oz/½ cup) buckwheat flour
1 teaspoon ground cinnamon
½ teaspoon ground ginger
½ teaspoon sea salt
125 ml (4 fl oz/½ cup) cold-pressed coconut oil
5 tablespoons pure maple syrup
¼ teaspoon vanilla powder or 1 teaspoon vanilla extract
125 ml (4 fl oz/½ cup) filtered water
50 g (2 oz/1 cup) coconut chips

—

Preheat the oven to 200°C/400°F/Gas mark 6 and line a baking tray with parchment paper.

Add the dry ingredients (apart from the coconut chips) to a large bowl. Stir until well mixed and set aside.

Melt the coconut oil, maple syrup and vanilla in a saucepan on a low heat. Stir through the water and then pour over the dry ingredients. Mix until well combined.

continued overleaf

Spread the granola out in a single layer on the baking tray and bake
for 20–30 minutes or until golden, stirring occasionally.

Towards the last few minutes of baking, scatter the coconut chips on
top, but keep an eye on them as they burn quickly.

Remove from the oven and cool. Pour into a large sealable glass jar
and store in the pantry. It can keep for a month if sealed.

MUESLI

MAKES 700 g
1 lb 9 oz/7 cups

NUT-FREE

I don't think our home-made muesli has ever looked exactly the same, as every time we make it, we use different grains, cereals, seeds and dried fruits depending on what we have on hand at the time. Having said that, we do have a general rule of thumb that we try to follow to achieve the right balance of flavours and textures. Contrary to our granola, this muesli is entirely raw, nut-free and unsweetened, apart from the addition of dried fruit. As this muesli isn't toasted, we prefer to add it to the bottom of a smoothie jar, like in our Upside-Down Breakfast (page 89), or serve it with our Strawberry Cashew Milk (page 108). This way it soaks up the liquid and becomes soft and slightly chewy, just like Bircher muesli.

* Pumpkin seeds, sunflower seeds, linseeds, sesame seeds and hemp seeds all work well.

** Sultanas, raisins, currants, cranberries, blueberries, goji berries, roughly chopped apricots, figs, prunes, dates, apple slices and banana chips all work well. However, make sure that they don't contain added sugars, preservatives or colourings. Alternatively, use freeze-dried fruit.

*** Barley, corn, rye, wheat, spelt, rice, millet, kamut, sorghum, quinoa, buckwheat and amaranth all work well.

180 g (6 oz/2 cups) rolled oats or a combination of rolled and jumbo oats (choose certified gluten-free if allergic)

150 g (5 oz/1 cup) raw seeds*

150 g (5 oz/1 cup) unsweetened dried fruit**

90 g (3¼ oz/1 cup) raw wholegrain flakes***

50 g (2 oz/1 cup) puffed wholegrains***

50 g (2 oz/1 cup) desiccated coconut (or unsweetened coconut chips)

1 teaspoon ground cinnamon

½ teaspoon ground ginger

Put all of the ingredients in a large bowl and stir until well mixed.

Pour into a large sealable glass jar and store in the pantry. The muesli can keep for months in the pantry, if sealed.

SIMPLE SMOOTHIES

One weekend every month, my dad invites us to brunch. It's his social meal of choice and one he takes seriously. There are at least three varieties of sourdough bread on the table (two sorts of rye and one with apricots studded into it), along with butter, jams and cheeses, no-flour banana pancakes – 'It's your recipe,' he proudly adds, every time – a large bowl of fruit salad, cappuccino and freshly squeezed orange juice. At times, there is even a pink birthday cake there, 'To celebrate that we are all gathered here!' And always, without exception, there is a large jug of his home-made smoothie on the table. He is not the most adventurous smoothie maker, but has found a few good ingredient combinations that he rotates to create a pink, purple or blue fruit smoothie.

We love Dad's smoothies, but we created this chapter with him in mind. 'Would Dad make this?' meant was it simple enough for him to try, although perhaps a little new and more daring in flavour. We have added spices or nut butter to a few of these smoothies and vegetables to some, but apart from that, they are quick, easy and pretty straightforward. All ingredients can be found in normal supermarkets and the recipes are simply mixed in a blender and poured into a glass.

So, while we hope that you will also try some of the more intriguing smoothies in this book, these recipes are all great as a starting point.

DAVID

KIDS' GREENIE

A trick to get children to eat more vegetables is to add them to smoothies. Blending vegetables with sweeter flavours disguises their taste and makes them more appealing. Frozen vegetables are the best option as they are milder in taste and often actually contain more nutrients than fresh vegetables (because they are frozen directly after being picked). Other plus sides are that they are generally cheaper, available all year round and obviously have a much longer shelf life. This green smoothie contains both broccoli and peas, yet has a sweet and fruity flavour due to the banana and a kick of freshness from the orange juice and ginger. We created this recipe to be child-friendly, but it is just as good for any adults who want to incorporate more vegetables into their lives.

—

1 ripe banana, peeled
50 g (2 oz/¼ cup) frozen broccoli florets
50 g (2 oz/⅓ cup) frozen peas
1 tablespoon linseeds
½ teaspoon fresh ginger, grated (or ¼ teaspoon ground ginger)
250 ml (8½ fl oz/1 cup) freshly squeezed orange juice (unsweetened and not from concentrate or from approx. 3 oranges)

—

Roughly chop the banana and add it to a blender along with the rest of the ingredients.

Blend on a high speed until completely smooth.

Pour into two medium-sized glass bottles or four small ones and serve with straws.

SIMPLE RASPBERRY SMOOTHIE

This is one of our ultimate go-to smoothies as the ingredients are basic and no superfoods are required. It looks pretty and tastes great, with no unusual flavours or acquired tastes. So it is something that all kids and non-smoothie-drinking adults usually enjoy! It has a fresh raspberry and yoghurt flavour with a zing of lemon and a touch of sweetness from the dates and coconut.

180 g (6 oz/1½ cups) frozen raspberries

4–5 soft dates, pitted

2 tablespoons desiccated coconut, unsweetened

250 g (9 oz/1 cup) plain unsweetened yoghurt (for a vegan alternative use coconut yoghurt or organic GMO-free soya yoghurt)

1 tablespoon lemon juice

100 ml (3½ fl oz/½ cup) filtered water, if needed

Put all of the ingredients in a blender and blend on a high speed until completely smooth. Depending on the strength of your blender, you may need to add a little water.

Taste and adjust the sweetness to your liking by adding more dates if necessary.

Pour into two medium-sized glass jars or a large one (as featured in the photo) and serve.

MOCHA
MORNING BUZZ

SERVES 1

NUT-FREE

Our chilled smoothie version of a morning cappuccino has the addition of dates for a little sweetness, a touch of cacao and some rolled oats to make it thicker and more comforting so you'll last longer on it. It's a real treat and has a very round flavour. We are leaving some leeway here with the amount of espresso and dates, so you can make it as potent or as sweet as you like.

On hot summer mornings, we fill our glass with ice before pouring over the blend and call it a Mochachino on the Rocks.

3–5 soft dates, pitted
2 teaspoons cacao powder
3 tablespoons rolled oats (choose certified gluten-free if allergic)
250 ml (8½ fl oz/1 cup) unsweetened plant milk
1–2 shots espresso (approx. 2–4 tablespoons)
1 teaspoon cold-pressed coconut oil
2 ice cubes

Put all of the ingredients in a blender and blend on a high speed until completely smooth.

Taste and adjust the sweetness and coffee flavour to your liking by adding more dates, espresso or milk, if necessary.

Pour into one medium-sized glass or cup (as featured in the photo) and enjoy right away. The swirl in the photo is simply a splash of extra plant milk stirred with a spoon.

GREENS FOR ALL

—

NUT-FREE

This is one of our absolute favourite green smoothies and yet it's so quick and easy to make, with only a few ingredients. The sweet and juicy pineapple balances the grassy flavour of the spinach perfectly, while the ginger provides a spicy punch. When you get equally obsessed with this combo as us, we can also recommend making Pineapple Greens (page 123) in the Juices chapter.

—

* If your pineapple isn't that sweet and juicy, you can always use more or add half a ripe banana.

150 g (5 oz/1 cup) ripe pineapple, peeled*
60 g (2 oz/1 cup) frozen spinach (organic if possible)
½ ripe avocado
juice of ½ lime
½–1 teaspoon fresh ginger, grated (or ¼–½ teaspoon ground ginger)
250 ml (8½ fl oz/1 cup) rice milk (or coconut water)

Roughly chop the pineapple and add it to a blender along with the rest of the ingredients.

Blend on a high speed until completely smooth. Taste and adjust the spiciness to your liking by adding more ginger if necessary.

Pour into two medium-sized glasses and serve or store in a large airtight glass bottle to take on a picnic (as featured in the photo).

GOODNIGHT SMOOTHIE

SERVES 1
or 2 small servings

Warm chamomile tea with honey is a good sleep aid and has been used for decades, but this creamy smoothie with a touch of warming spices is just as effective. Bananas and almonds are rich in magnesium, which is an antidote to stress and a powerful relaxation mineral, while nutmeg is a sedative. Therefore, by maximizing your intake of natural magnesium just before bedtime, you're more likely to sleep better.

You can also add a quality magnesium powder supplement (which you can find at all good health food stores) if you suffer from insomnia or your child has trouble sleeping or suffers from growing pains. Sleep tight!

1 ripe banana, peeled
2 tablespoons raw almonds (pre-soaked if possible)
1 tablespoon linseeds
pinch ground nutmeg
125–250 ml (4–8½ fl oz/½–1 cup) filtered water
1 teaspoon cold-pressed coconut oil
½ teaspoon ground vanilla or vanilla extract

Roughly chop the banana and add it to a blender along with the rest of the ingredients.

Blend on a high speed until completely smooth. Taste and adjust the consistency to your liking by adding more water if necessary.

Pour into a medium-sized glass (as featured in the photo) or two small ones and serve at room temperature to avoid shocking your body right before bedtime.

TIP: *Brown rice protein powder is also rich in magnesium and is a great addition to increase the overall nutritional value and keep you from waking up hungry during the night.*

SUPERBERRY & FENNEL SMOOTHIE

SERVES 2
or 1 large serving

Living in a country with distinct seasons, we have access to mostly imported fruit and vegetables during the winter months. Therefore, we always make sure to stock up on loads of frozen local berries so we can at least make delicious smoothies all year round. Berries are low in sugar, contain high amounts of antioxidants (which protect our cells from damage caused by free radicals) and are one of our favourite ingredients, not only in smoothies. In this smoothie, we simply use a bag of mixed berries (usually a mix of strawberries, raspberries, blueberries and blackcurrants) along with an avocado for creaminess, ginger for some bite, orange as a sweetener and fennel for healthy cleansing properties. It doesn't, however, taste healthy at all, just very fresh! You can always add a banana if you prefer it sweeter.

1 orange (blood orange if possible), peeled
½ small fennel bulb, trimmed (approx. 50–70 g/2–2½ oz)
½ ripe avocado, stone removed
150 g (5 oz/1 cup) frozen mixed berries
½–1 teaspoon fresh ginger, grated (or ¼–½ teaspoon ground ginger)
250 ml (8½ fl oz/1 cup) almond milk (or unsweetened milk of choice)

Roughly chop the orange and fennel and add them to a blender along with the flesh of the avocado and the rest of the ingredients.

Blend on a high speed until completely smooth. Taste and adjust the spiciness to your liking by adding more ginger if necessary.

Pour into two medium-sized glass jars or a large one (as featured in the photo) and serve with straws.

AVOCADO, MANGO & LIME SMOOTHIE

SERVES 2

—

NUT-FREE

Avocados feature in several of our smoothies in this book as they create a silky smooth and creamy texture without the need for bananas or dairy products. However, in this creamy smoothie, avocado is no longer a mere accessory, rather the star ingredient! We combine it with a generous amount of lime juice for freshness, as well as mango and dates for sweetness. The result is an ultra-lush and creamy smoothie with a flavour that reminds us of Key lime pie.

—

If using frozen mango, you can always add a dash of freshly squeezed orange juice (unsweetened and not from concentrate) to the blender for extra sweetness.

1 ripe avocado, stone removed

½ ripe mango, stone removed (or frozen*) (approx. 100 g/3½ oz/ ½ cup mango flesh)

2–4 soft dried dates, pitted

250 ml (8½ fl oz/1 cup) filtered water

juice of 1–2 limes

Add the avocado and mango flesh to a blender along with the rest of the ingredients.

Blend on a high speed until completely smooth.

Taste and adjust the sweetness and sourness to your liking by adding more dates and/or lime juice if necessary.

Pour into two medium-sized glasses (one of which is featured in the photo) and serve cold.

TROPICALIA

SERVES 2
—

NUT-FREE

Personally, I don't think melons are *that great* in smoothies. David often tries to convince me by telling me how packed they are with liquid: 'They practically came to this earth to be liquefied.' But I am just of the opinion that they are much yummier chewed on. This is, however, one melon smoothie recipe that we both could agree on. Mango, passion fruit and lime make it very fruity, sweet, tropical and super-refreshing. It truly has the power to make even the most obnoxious melon smoothie opponent crave for more.

LUISE

---

1 orange, peeled

½ small honeydew (or cantaloupe) melon, seeds removed (approx. 300 g/10½ oz/2 cups melon flesh)

½ ripe mango, stone removed (or frozen) (approx. 100 g/3½ oz/½ cup mango flesh)

1 passion fruit or ½ golden kiwi fruit

juice of ½ lime

Roughly chop the orange and add it to a blender along with the flesh of the melon and mango, the pulp of the passion fruit and the lime juice.

Blend on a high speed until completely smooth.

Pour into two medium-sized glasses (one of which is featured in the photo) and serve cold.

Top left: Banana Snickers Shake; *top middle:* Simple Raspberry Smoothie; *middle left:* Tropicalia; *middle right:* Greens for All; *bottom right:* Beans, Beets and Blues

BANANA SNICKERS SHAKE

SERVES 2

Voilà, the recipe for the ultimate afternoon pick-me-up! It's a quick and easy smoothie that tastes like a Snickers chocolate bar (well, almost anyway), only healthy! Peanuts are rich in healthy monounsaturated fatty acids and energy, thus will keep you going until dinner. This is our son's number one favourite drink and just 10 seconds after taking this photo, he had already poured half the shake into his mouth while the rest was spilled all over that snazzy little denim shirt of his.

If you don't make our home-made peanut butter, choose a quality peanut butter brand that contains only toasted (or raw) organic peanuts and salt. Avoid those with hydrogenated oils, refined sugar and other additives.

TIP: *For a more nutritious and substantial shake, try adding 1 tablespoon protein powder (from peas, hemp seeds, brown rice or whey).*

2 frozen bananas (page 22)
4 tablespoons peanut butter (see Nut Butter, page 26)*
2 tablespoons cacao powder
pinch sea salt
250 ml (8½ fl oz/1 cup) filtered water

Put all of the ingredients in a blender and blend on a high speed until completely smooth.

Taste and adjust the saltiness to your liking, by adding more salt if necessary.

Pour into two medium-sized glass bottles (one of which is featured in the photo) and serve with straws.

STRAWBERRY POMPOM

We realized how well basil and strawberries tasted together when we combined them in a lentil salad in our first book. Ever since then, I always top my strawberry rye sandwiches with basil leaves, and we often add a few of them to our strawberry smoothies as they create more body. Here we also add some pomegranate seeds for a sweet, juicy and fresh twist. It's a real crowd-pleaser this one. Enjoy!

DAVID

150 g (5 oz/1 cup) frozen strawberries (or fresh) (organic if possible)
1 ripe banana, peeled (or frozen, if using fresh strawberries)
seeds of ½ pomegranate (approx. 90 g/3¼ oz/½ cup)
4–6 fresh basil leaves
pinch vanilla powder or ½ teaspoon vanilla extract
250 ml (8½ fl oz/1 cup) oat milk (or almond milk)

Put all of the ingredients in a blender and blend on a high speed until completely smooth.

Taste and adjust the basil flavour to your liking by adding more leaves, if necessary.

Pour into two medium-sized glasses and serve.

THREE POST-WORKOUT SMOOTHIES

While writing this book, inevitably we have found that smoothies can be the answer to almost every meal situation and time of the day. However, if we were to choose one occasion when smoothies are optimal, it would have to be after physical exercise. When you are too tired to cook a meal, there is no quicker way to refill your body with energy. We have created three different post-workout smoothies here with ingredients that not only optimize the recovery after various types of physical exercise, but also taste incredible.

GREEN REHYDRATION
POST-CARDIO

SERVES 2
or 1 large serving

—

NUT-FREE

Celery contains anti-inflammatory properties and is a great source of sodium, while bananas are rich in potassium and spinach is high in magnesium – all of which are electrolytes that you lose when you sweat. Together with the hydrating coconut water and protein from the pea powder, they are the perfect ingredients to help your body recover and rehydrate after a workout. The lime and ginger, on the other hand, provide a fresh boost in flavour.

—

1 celery stalk (with leaves) (organic if possible)
1 frozen banana (page 22)
1 handful spinach (or any other leafy greens) (organic if possible)
1 tablespoon pea protein powder (or another high-quality protein powder)
½ teaspoon fresh ginger, grated (or ¼ teaspoon ground ginger)
250 ml (8½ fl oz/1 cup) coconut water
juice of ½ lime

—

TIP: *Read more about protein powders on page 13.*

Depending on the strength of your blender, roughly or finely chop the celery and add it to the blender along with the rest of the ingredients.

Blend on a high speed until completely smooth.

Pour into two medium-sized glasses and serve, or store in a large airtight glass bottle to pack into your gym bag.

continued overleaf

PURPLE PERFORMANCE
PRE- AND POST-WORKOUT

Beets (and other nitrate-rich vegetables) improve blood and oxygen flow in muscles and prompt them to use the oxygen more efficiently. Sour cherries are rich in antioxidants and help the body to recover from intense training, as well as reducing delayed-onset muscle pain. Drink beetroot and sour cherry juices and smoothies regularly to gain the physical benefits.

---

1 small raw beetroot, peeled (approx. 80 g/3 oz)
1 tablespoon dried sour cherries or sour cherry powder (or goji berries)
60 g (2 oz/½ cup) frozen raspberries
1 ripe banana, peeled
1 tablespoon hemp seeds or hemp protein powder (or more if you like)
½–1 teaspoon fresh ginger, grated (or ¼–½ teaspoon ground ginger)
350 ml (12 fl oz/1½ cups) almond milk (or unsweetened milk of choice)
1–2 tablespoons lemon juice

Depending on the strength of your blender, roughly chop or grate the beetroot and add it to the blender along with the rest of the ingredients.

Blend on a high speed until completely smooth. Taste and adjust the spiciness and sourness to your liking by adding more ginger or lemon juice if necessary.

Pour into two medium-sized glasses and serve, or store in a large airtight glass bottle to pack into your gym bag (as featured in the photo).

—
TIP: *Read more about protein powders on page 13.*

continued overleaf

BLUEBERRY POWER
POST-STRENGTH TRAINING

SERVES 2
or 1 large serving
—

Focussing on fuelling your muscles after strength training is almost as important as the workout itself, because it helps your muscles to recover and grow. The body needs a combination of carbohydrates and proteins right after exercise and this smoothie has got those covered! A protein smoothie doesn't sound very sexy, but this drink actually tastes a lot like a bottled blueberry pie. You can use any protein powder you wish, but look for a high-quality one with only a few pure ingredients. You can always ask your local health food store for advice.

1 ripe banana, peeled
150 g (5 oz/1 cup) frozen blueberries
2 tablespoons Nut Butter (page 26)
1 tablespoon pumpkin seeds
1 tablespoon whey protein powder (or other protein powder of choice)
¼ teaspoon ground cardamom
250 ml (8½ fl oz/1 cup) almond milk (or unsweetened milk of choice)

Roughly chop the banana and add it to a blender along with the rest of the ingredients.

Blend on a high speed until completely smooth.

Pour into two medium-sized glasses and serve, or store in a large airtight glass bottle to pack into your gym bag.

TIP: *Read more about protein powders on page 13.*

SHOWSTOPPERS

—

Smoothies are fantastic on their own – quick to make, easy to vary, filled with healthy fruit and vegetables and, most importantly, delicious to drink. It wasn't like we intended to take something simple and make it more complicated. We just realized, around our 537th smoothie, that there were a few methods we could use to make our smoothies even better. So in this chapter we serve them in bowls with lots of granola and fresh fruit on top; we layer them in high glasses together with chia pudding, yoghurt or nut butter; we pour them over mashed fresh berries to create beautiful swirls of colour; and we make amazing two-coloured smoothies from one single smoothie batch. This way we get a variation in texture and flavour, and it often also makes a more substantial meal. Not to mention, they all look showstopping! These are not smoothies that you keep in your gym bag, but ones you can proudly serve to friends who pop over. In contrast to their impressive look, most of the recipes in this chapter are not difficult to make at all. They of course take a little more preparation than in the Simple Smoothies chapter, but we promise that they are worth it. Use these recipes as a start and, before you know it, you will be creating showstopping smoothies of your own.

MANGO & CHIA PARFAIT

SERVES 2

NUT-FREE

When mangos are in season and picked ripe, they taste unreal – so sweet and juicy. When we were travelling around Australia we just couldn't stop feasting on them. We wanted to bottle that flavour and thus we came up with this exotic tropical delight. Layers of a pearly white and creamy coconut chia pudding with the aromatic floral tones of vanilla are marbled with fresh and tangy passion fruit pulp and a sweet and juicy mango smoothie. Ginger and lime add a spicy and zingy punch, while buckwheat and tahini add body, volume and a natural calcium boost. This one is a real showstopper. Indulge!

* If using frozen mango, you can always add a dash of freshly squeezed orange juice (unsweetened and not from concentrate) to the blender for extra sweetness.

FOR THE CHIA PUDDING LAYER
250 ml (8½ fl oz/1 cup) Coconut Chia Pudding (made with white chia seeds and coconut drinking milk or tinned coconut milk) (page 28)

FOR THE MANGO SMOOTHIE LAYER
1 ripe mango, stone removed (or frozen, thawed*) (approx. 200 g/7 oz/1 cup mango flesh)

2 passion fruit or 1 golden kiwi fruit

2 tablespoons raw buckwheat (pre-soaked if possible)

1 teaspoon hulled tahini

½ teaspoon fresh ginger, grated (or ¼ teaspoon ground ginger)

juice of ½ lime

TO SERVE
2 passion fruit or golden kiwi fruit, pulp (mashed)

mango flesh, finely chopped

toasted coconut chips

Add the mango flesh and passion fruit or kiwi fruit pulp to a blender along with the rest of the mango smoothie layer ingredients.

Blend on a high speed until completely smooth.

Spoon half of the chia pudding into the base of two medium-sized glasses (one of which is featured in the photo).

Cover with a layer of the mashed passion or kiwi fruit pulp and half of the mango smoothie. For a beautiful artistic look, make messy uneven layers. Repeat with the rest of the chia pudding, more passion fruit pulp and the remaining mango smoothie.

Serve the parfait cold with some chopped mango and passion fruit pulp, and a sprinkling of coconut chips.

PINK BREAKFAST BOWL

SERVES 2
or 1 large serving
—

Even though smoothies are often served in glasses, bottles or jars, they can also be presented in bowls and eaten with spoons. In fact, this makes them feel like proper meals and provides a larger surface area for toppings, which is always a bonus. This creation is slightly thicker than a normal smoothie and contains protein powder to make it a complete breakfast, and such a pretty one at that.

---

250 ml (8½ fl oz/1 cup) oat milk (or almond milk)
1 frozen banana (page 22)
120 g (4 oz/1 cup) frozen raspberries
60 g (2 oz/½ cup) frozen or fresh redcurrants (or lingonberries)
2 tablespoons protein powder (brown rice, hemp, pea or whey)
1 tablespoon Nut Butter (page 26)
1 tablespoon maca powder
1 tablespoon lemon juice
FOR THE TOPPING
hemp seeds or bee pollen
linseeds
toasted coconut chips
fresh blackberries, redcurrants and blackcurrants
edible pansies, optional

Add half of the milk to a blender along with the rest of the ingredients.

Blend on a high speed until completely smooth, adding more milk if needed.

Pour into two small bowls or a medium-sized one (as featured in the photo). Finish with a sprinkling of seeds and coconut chips, as well as a few berries and pansies, and serve.

PEANUT BUTTER & JAM MILKSHAKE

This liquid version of the classic peanut butter and jam sandwich is a revelation! It's easy to prepare, outrageously tasty and the strawberries create a beautiful marbled effect, while the lime adds a fresh twist. It might seem easier to just throw the strawberries in the blender with the rest of the ingredients, but please respect the layers, they are what takes this milkshake to the next level.

FOR THE PEANUT BUTTER MILKSHAKE
1 ripe banana, peeled
3 tablespoons quality peanut butter (or any other Nut Butter, page 26)
250 ml (8½ fl oz/1 cup) oat milk (or milk of choice)
2–3 ice cubes

TO SERVE
fresh strawberries, tops removed (organic if possible)
juice of ½ lime

Put all of the peanut butter milkshake ingredients in a blender and blend on a high speed until completely smooth.

Cut the strawberries into quarters and lightly mash them with a fork before dividing them between two medium-sized glasses or putting them in a large one (as featured in the photo). Squeeze the lime juice over the strawberries and muddle them with the back of a spoon to release some of their juices.

Pour the peanut butter milkshake on top of the muddled strawberries and serve.

CHIA & RASPBERRY PUDDING

This raspberry variation of a chia pudding is simple, satisfying and very delicious as a breakfast or snack. You could even serve it for dessert if you sweeten it slightly by blending dates with the milk. It is also perfect as a quick, on-the-go breakfast to keep in the fridge. Add whatever toppings you prefer. We like to add some nut butter as it balances out the sweet and tangy fruit flavours.

—

* You can replace the raspberries with other berries or mashed fruit, and the milk with freshly squeezed juice.

—

120 g (4 oz/1 cup) fresh ripe raspberries (or frozen, thawed)*
3 tablespoons desiccated coconut
3 tablespoons black chia seeds
½ teaspoon ground vanilla or vanilla extract
250 ml (8½ fl oz/1 cup) plant milk of choice
FOR THE TOPPING
hazelnut butter (or any other Nut Butter, page 26)
green kiwi fruit, chopped
fresh raspberries and blackberries
fresh mint leaves
hemp seeds

—

Put the raspberries in a bowl and mash them with a fork. Stir in the coconut, chia seeds and vanilla and then pour over the milk and mix until well combined. Stir every now and again for the first 10 minutes to prevent lumps from forming.

Set aside to soak in the fridge for at least 30 minutes or overnight. The pudding is ready when the consistency is thick and jelly-like.

Spoon into two medium-sized glass jars or a large one. Cover with a layer of nut butter and finish with the fruit, a few mint leaves and a sprinkling of hemp seeds. It can keep for a couple of days in the fridge (without the toppings), if unopened.

GREEN GOODNESS BOWL

SERVES 2
or 1 large serving

Frozen vegetables are not exactly the chicest of ingredients as much of their texture is lost when they are thawed. But they are perfect in smoothies as they are often cheaper, available all year round and make them thicker than fresh vegetables do. In this smoothie bowl, the sweet flavour of the pear and dates balances out the savoury taste of the vegetables just beautifully. The avocado adds creaminess, while the ginger, lime and coconut water provide a fresh twist. I add algae or grass powders to my bowl as they provide extra nutrients and have a stunning deep green colour. Beware, though, as they can become overpowering in flavour. Start with just ½ teaspoon and then add more if you prefer.

LUISE

1 medium-sized ripe pear, seeds removed (approx. 130–150 g/4½–5 oz)

½ ripe avocado, stone removed

50 g (2 oz/½ cup) frozen broccoli florets

50 g (2 oz/¾ cup) frozen spinach (organic if possible)

2–4 soft dates, pitted

½–1 teaspoon fresh ginger, grated (or ¼–½ teaspoon ground ginger)

½–1 teaspoon spirulina powder (or chlorella, wheatgrass or barley grass)

250 ml (8½ fl oz/1 cup) coconut water (or milk of choice)

juice of ½ lime

FOR THE TOPPING

pistachio nuts, finely chopped

toasted raw buckwheat*

desiccated coconut

hemp seeds or bee pollen

green kiwi fruit, finely chopped

passion fruit or golden kiwi fruit, pulp (mashed)

edible flowers, optional

* Toast raw (greenish) buckwheat in a dry frying pan (skillet) on a medium heat for approx. 5 minutes or until golden. If you have a sweet tooth, try adding a drizzle of pure maple syrup to the pan. You can also purchase sprouted and dehydrated crunchy buckwheat in health food stores.

Roughly chop the pear and add it to a blender along with the flesh of the avocado and the rest of the ingredients. Blend on a high speed until completely smooth.

Taste and adjust the sweetness and spiciness to your liking by adding more dates or ginger if necessary, as well as more spirulina if you prefer. Pour into two small bowls or a large one (as featured in the photo). Finish with a sprinkling of the nuts, buckwheat, coconut and seeds, as well as the fruit and flowers, and serve.

NUTS & BLUES

Nut-based smoothies have always been one of our absolute favourites, with their rich, creamy, sweet and satisfying flavour. To prevent the nutty taste from being too overpowering in this smoothie, we add some fresh blueberries to the bottom of the glasses or glass bottle. They balance out the flavours and at the same time create beautiful blue patterns in the smoothie. For extra finesse, we like to finish with a sprinkling of roughly chopped toasted salted nuts.

2 ripe bananas, peeled (use frozen bananas for a thicker consistency)
½ ripe avocado, stone removed
3 tablespoons hazelnut butter (or any other Nut Butter, page 26)
1 tablespoon cacao powder
375 ml (13 fl oz/1½ cups) cold almond milk
pinch sea salt
TO SERVE
fresh blueberries (or frozen, thawed)
toasted, salted almonds or hazelnuts, roughly chopped*

* To toast the nuts, take the roughly chopped raw nuts and toast them in a dry frying pan (skillet) on a medium heat with a pinch of sea salt for approx. 5 minutes or until golden. If you have a sweet tooth, try adding some cold-pressed coconut oil, a drizzle of pure maple syrup and a pinch of sea salt to the pan (½ teaspoon each of the coconut oil and maple syrup to every 2 tablespoons of nuts).

Roughly chop the bananas and add to a blender along with the flesh of the avocado and the rest of the ingredients.

Blend on a high speed until completely smooth.

Divide the blueberries between two medium-sized glasses or put them in a large glass bottle (as featured in the photo). Muddle them slightly with the back of a spoon to release some of their juices.

Pour the nut smoothie on top of the muddled blueberries, finish with a sprinkling of the nuts and serve.

GOJI, MANGO & TURMERIC SMOOTHIE

There is a deli around the corner from where we live in Stockholm that used to serve a goji berry smoothie that was so addictive that we just had to make our own version of it. Goji berries have been used in traditional Chinese medicine for thousands of years and are an excellent source of antioxidants. Combined with the orange and carrot juice, they make a smoothie that is packed with vitamin C and betacarotene to help protect against immune system deficiencies. The flavour of this smoothie is quite sweet with a wide variety of fruity tones – very unique! To balance the sweetness we also make it quite spicy with a big chunk of ginger, a touch of turmeric and pinch of black pepper. These ingredients also add some great anti-inflammatory properties to the drink.

1 orange, peeled and roughly chopped

1 ripe mango, stone removed (or frozen, thawed) (approx. 150 g/5 oz/ 1 cup mango flesh)

40 g (1½ oz/⅓ cup) dried goji berries (organic if possible)

½–1 teaspoon fresh ginger, grated (or ¼–½ teaspoon ground ginger)

1 teaspoon fresh turmeric, grated (or ½ teaspoon ground turmeric)

250 ml (8½ fl oz/1 cup) freshly squeezed carrot juice (4–5 carrots) (or brown rice milk)

pinch black pepper

2 tablespoons black chia seeds

Place all of the ingredients except the chia seeds in a blender. Blend on a high speed until completely smooth. Taste and adjust the spiciness to your liking by adding more ginger if necessary.

Pour into two medium-sized glasses. Stir in the chia seeds and serve chilled.

CHOCOLATE VELVET

SERVES 2
—

We have a recipe for a chocolate and beetroot cake in our first book. It's a very popular cake and it's easy to understand why, given that the decadent flavour of chocolate and earthy undertones of beetroot are a match made in heaven. When we created this smoothie recipe we wanted to make a liquid version of that cake. We use avocado to create a smooth, creamy consistency, dates for sweetness and blackberries for a fresh twist.

———

1 small raw beetroot, peeled (approx. 80 g/3 oz)

½ ripe avocado, stone removed

75 g (2½ oz/½ cup) frozen blackberries

5–8 soft dates, pitted

2 tablespoons cacao powder

350 ml (12 fl oz/1½ cups) organic GMO-free soya milk (or unsweetened almond milk)

FOR THE TOPPING

cacao powder

———

Depending on the strength of your blender, roughly chop or grate the beetroot and add it to the blender along with the flesh of the avocado and the rest of the ingredients.

Blend on a high speed until completely smooth. Taste and adjust the sweetness to your liking by adding more dates if necessary.

Pour into two medium-sized glasses (one of which is featured in the photo), dust with cacao powder and serve.

ORANGE SESAME SMOOTHIE WITH MUDDLED RASPBERRIES

SERVES 2

NUT-FREE

Here we mix sesame seed cream with juicy oranges and a spoonful of spicy cinnamon to create a very special and rather Moroccan-tasting smoothie. We then pour it over fresh muddled raspberries. Not only do the raspberries visually enhance this drink, they also add a delicious twist in flavour as you work your way to the bottom of the glass jar.

2 oranges, peeled
500 ml (17 fl oz/2 cups) Sesame Seed Cream (see note on page 110)
2–4 soft dates, pitted
1 teaspoon ground cinnamon
pinch sea salt
TO SERVE
fresh raspberries (or frozen, thawed)
ground cinnamon

Roughly chop the oranges and add them to a blender along with the sesame seed cream and the rest of the ingredients.

Blend on a high speed until completely smooth. Taste and adjust the sweetness to your liking by adding more dates if necessary.

Divide the raspberries between two medium-sized glass jars (one of which is featured in the photo) and muddle them slightly with the back of a spoon to release some of their juices.

Pour the sesame smoothie on top of the muddled raspberries, finish with a sprinkling of cinnamon and serve.

AÇAÍ BOWL
EXTRA EVERYTHING!

SERVES 2
or 1 large serving

Açaí, the Amazonian superberries, have to be frozen or freeze-dried immediately after picking to maintain their potency. We always try to encourage choosing locally grown ingredients but we just couldn't write a book about smoothies and not include one açaí recipe. If you try it you'll understand why! The earthy flavours taste so good when mixed with strawberries, sweet banana and honey. Don't be shy with the toppings here. We add heaps of fresh fruit for sweetness, granola for crunch, nut butter for richness and edible flowers to pretend that we are in Brazil when eating this delectable delight!

* *Frozen açaí pulp is usually sold in large packs that can be hard for the blender to crush. If that is the case, you can just crush the frozen pulp with the back of a knife before adding it to the blender.*

1 pack (100 g/3½ oz) frozen açaí pulp* (or 2 tablespoons freeze-dried açaí powder plus 100 g/4 oz/¾ cup frozen blueberries)

150 g (5 oz/1 cup) frozen strawberries (organic if possible)

1 frozen banana (page 22)

2 tablespoons quality raw honey

125 ml (4 fl oz/½ cup) oat or almond milk

FOR THE TOPPING

fresh fruit (a mix of thinly sliced red apple and green kiwi fruit, chopped figs, berries and passion fruit pulp)

Coconut & Buckwheat granola (page 29)

desiccated coconut

Nut Butter (page 26)

edible flowers, optional

Put all of the ingredients for the açaí bowl in a blender and blend on a high speed until completely smooth.

Pour into two small bowls or a medium-sized one, top with fresh fruit and finish with a sprinkling of granola and coconut, a dollop of the butter and a few edible flowers and serve.

NOTE: The photo features a double recipe.

GREEN GAZPACHO SMOOTHIE

SERVES 2
or 4 small servings

NUT-FREE

Calling a gazpacho a smoothie might seem like a far stretch. But if you think about it, this gazpacho follows the same method as our other smoothies, albeit with a little less liquid and purely savoury ingredients. This is a really pleasant light yet satisfying lunch and perfect on a really hot day. By serving it in sealable glass jars, it's also ideal for a picnic.

---

1 yellow or green (bell) pepper, core and seeds removed (organic if possible)
2 celery stalks (with leaves) (organic if possible)
10 cm (4 in) piece cucumber (organic if possible)
1 handful fresh parsley, stems included
4 fresh chives
½ garlic clove
1 ripe avocado, stone removed
1 tablespoon cold-pressed extra virgin olive oil
1 tablespoon organic unfiltered apple cider vinegar
pinch sea salt
pinch black pepper
TO SERVE
plain unsweetened yoghurt (optional)
cold-pressed extra virgin olive oil
fresh parsley, chopped
cayenne pepper

Roughly chop the pepper, celery, cucumber, parsley, chives and garlic and add them to a blender along with the flesh of the avocado and the rest of the ingredients.

Blend on a high speed until completely smooth like the consistency of a soup. Taste and adjust the flavours to your liking by adding more oil, vinegar, salt or pepper if necessary.

Pour into two medium-sized sealable glass jars or four small ones (three of which are featured in the photo). Serve cold with a swirl of the yoghurt (if using) and oil, as well as a sprinkling of parsley and a pinch of cayenne pepper.

GRAB & GO
BLACKBERRY OATS

SERVES 2
or 1 large serving

—

NUT-FREE

This is the ultimate breakfast for late sleepers. Maximize your time in bed by preparing the smoothie the night before and storing it in a sealable glass jar in the fridge. That way, in the morning all you have to do is grab it and go. The quickest breakfast ever! The oats and chia seeds will keep you going and the combination of blackberries, honey and vanilla is super-tasty.

---

150 g (5 oz/1 cup) fresh ripe blackberries (or frozen, thawed)

250 g (9 oz/1 cup) plain unsweetened yoghurt (for a vegan alternative use coconut yoghurt or organic GMO-free soya yoghurt)

1–2 tablespoons quality raw honey

½ teaspoon ground vanilla or vanilla extract

45 g (1½ oz/½ cup) rolled oats (choose certified gluten-free if allergic)

2 tablespoons black chia seeds

TO SERVE

slices of a firm but ripe banana

Put the blackberries, yoghurt, honey and vanilla in a blender and blend on a high speed until completely smooth.

Taste and adjust the sweetness to your liking by adding more honey if necessary.

Pour into a bowl and stir in the oats and chia seeds. Arrange the banana slices around the inside of two sealable medium-sized glass jars or a large one (as featured in the photo).

Pour the smoothie on top and serve chilled (to give the oats and chia seeds a chance to soak) with spoons. Alternatively, store in the fridge overnight to grab on your way out the next morning. It can keep for a couple of days in the fridge, if unopened.

UPSIDE-DOWN BREAKFAST

This is a favourite method of ours where we place toppings (muesli, granola, rolled oats, puffed grains or nuts) at the bottom of a glass jar and then cover them with a few spoonfuls of yoghurt, followed by a smoothie. It's a delicious way to have breakfast – and looks spectacular too. In this recipe we use muesli and Greek yoghurt for the bottom two layers and a simple but flavoursome berry & spinach smoothie on top, but feel free to try this technique with some of the other smoothies in the Simple Smoothies chapter.

FOR THE BERRY & SPINACH SMOOTHIE
1 ripe banana, peeled
1 handful fresh baby spinach, rinsed
75 g/½ cup frozen or fresh strawberries (organic if possible)
75 g/½ cup frozen blueberries
½ teaspoon ground cardamom
250 ml (8½ fl oz/1 cup) oat milk or almond milk (unsweetened)
FOR THE BASE LAYERS
150 g (5 oz/1 cup) Muesli (page 31)
250 g (9 oz/1 cup) full-fat plain unsweetened Greek yoghurt (for a vegan alternative use coconut yoghurt or GMO-free soya yoghurt)

Roughly chop the banana and add to a blender along with the rest of the berry & spinach smoothie ingredients. Blend on a high speed until completely smooth.

Divide the muesli between four medium-sized glass jars or two large ones (one of which is featured in the photo). Spoon the yoghurt over the muesli in each glass jar. Pour the berry smoothie layer on top of the yoghurt, top with chopped fruit of your choice and serve.

CREAMY PEACH MELBA

SERVES 2
—

This is our liquid interpretation of the classic dessert peach Melba, combining peaches and raspberries in two beautiful layers. Although it's not as sweet as the original dessert, it's very fruity and also creamy, thanks to the addition of tahini. Even though it has two layers, you only need one quantity of smoothie ingredients to make it. Simply start by making the peach layer, divide half of it between two glass jars, then blend the rest with the raspberries to get the pink layer.

FOR THE PEACH LAYER

3 medium-sized ripe peaches, (approx. 300 g/10 oz), stones removed (or 1 × 400 g/14 oz tin sliced peaches in clear fruit juice, drained) (organic if possible)

½ frozen banana (page 22)

2 tablespoons hulled tahini

125 ml (4 fl oz/½ cup) oat or almond milk

1 tablespoon lemon juice

½ teaspoon ground vanilla or vanilla extract

2 ice cubes

FOR THE RASPBERRY LAYER

120 g (4 oz/1 cup) frozen raspberries

FOR THE TOPPING

thin slices of a firm but ripe peach

desiccated coconut

hemp seeds, chia seeds or bee pollen

Roughly chop the peaches and add them to a blender along with the rest of the peach layer ingredients.

Blend on a high speed until completely smooth.

Divide half of the peach layer smoothie between two medium-sized glass jars (as featured in the photo), leaving the other half in the blender. Add the raspberries to the blender and blend until they are fully incorporated and the mixture turns pink.

Slowly pour the raspberry layer on top of the peach layer, working your way from the outside to the inside of the glass jar (as the raspberry layer is heavier). To create a marbled effect, simply run the back of a teaspoon up and down along the inside of the glass jar. Be careful not to mix too much or the layers will blend into one. Finish with a few peach slices, as well as a sprinkling of coconut and seeds.

PUMPKIN PIE SMOOTHIE

SERVES 2
or 4 small servings

Summer is obviously our favourite season to indulge in smoothies, but autumn and winter also offer fruit and vegetables that are great. Take pumpkins and squashes for instance. When roasted and mixed into a purée, they have the perfect texture and sweetness for smoothies and can be used as an alternative to banana. Here we have added all the classic pumpkin pie spices to create a lush drink that looks beautiful with a little extra purée at the bottom of the glass. With the leftover purée you can make a soup, stir it through a risotto, use it in place of sweet potato in our Sweet Potato Gnocchi or even in our delicious Pumpkin and Almond Waffles (see *Green Kitchen Travels*). You can also use tinned pumpkin purée for this smoothie, in which case you can skip the first two paragraphs of the recipe method.

FOR THE PUMPKIN PURÉE

1 small Hokkaido pumpkin, red kuri squash or butternut squash
(or 1 × 400 g/14 oz tin pumpkin purée)

FOR THE SPICED PUMPKIN SMOOTHIE

4 tablespoons pumpkin purée

2–4 soft dates, pitted

¼ teaspoon ground cinnamon

¼ teaspoon ground ginger

pinch ground nutmeg

pinch ground cloves

250 ml (8½ fl oz/1 cup) walnut, almond & sesame milk (see Basic Nut Milk, page 106, or milk of choice)

pinch sea salt

TO SERVE

pumpkin purée

continued overleaf

To make the pumpkin purée, preheat the oven to 200°C/400°F/ Gas mark 6 and line a baking tray with parchment paper. Cut the pumpkin into quarters, scoop out the seeds and fibrous strings and place cut-side down on the baking tray. Bake for approx. 25–45 minutes (depending on the size of the pumpkin) or until the skin is golden and bubbled and the flesh is tender. Set aside to cool.

Spoon the flesh of the pumpkin into a food processor and process on a high speed until completely smooth. Store in the fridge in an airtight container for up to 5 days, or in the freezer.

When ready to make the smoothie, add 4 tablespoons of the fresh or tinned pumpkin purée to a blender with all of the spiced pumpkin smoothie ingredients and blend on a high speed until completely smooth. Taste and adjust the sweetness to your liking by adding more dates if necessary.

Add a generous dollop of the purée to the base of two medium-sized glasses or four small ones (two of which are featured in the photo). Pour the pumpkin smoothie on top and serve cold.

BEANS, BEETS & BLUES

Between August and September, the Swedish forests are overflowing with blueberries. We only need to take one step off the road leading to our family's summerhouse to find ourselves in a field of blue gems. In this smoothie, the combination of beetroot, blueberries and cinnamon gives it a fantastic earthy berry flavour. And to that we add white beans! It might sound like an odd ingredient but the beans don't affect the flavour, they just make the smoothie thicker and add extra protein. The smoothie is then topped and swirled with yoghurt, which makes it look stunning and become even more nourishing.

½ raw beetroot, peeled (approx. 50 g/2 oz)

1 ripe banana, peeled

150 g (5 oz/1 cup) frozen blueberries (plus extra for serving)

90 g (3 oz/½ cup) cooked white beans (rinse if using canned)

juice and zest of ½ lemon

½ teaspoon ground cinnamon

200 ml (7 fl oz/¾ cup) coconut water (or drinking water)

TO SERVE

500 ml/2 cups coconut yoghurt or Greek yoghurt

TIP: We use frozen blueberries in this recipe, but if you find yourself in a field of fresh ones, you should definitely use them instead. In that case, swap the fresh banana for a frozen one, or simply add a few ice cubes to keep the smoothie chilled.

Depending on the strength of your blender, roughly chop or grate the beetroot, roughly chop the banana and add them to a blender along with the rest of the ingredients.

Blend on a high speed until completely smooth. Pour into four medium-sized glasses, filling them about halfway. Fill up with yoghurt, working your way from the outside to the inside of the glass (as the yoghurt is heavier). Run a spoon around the inside edges of the glasses to create a marbled effect and top with extra blueberries (decorate with edible petals for extra va-va-voom).

photo overleaf

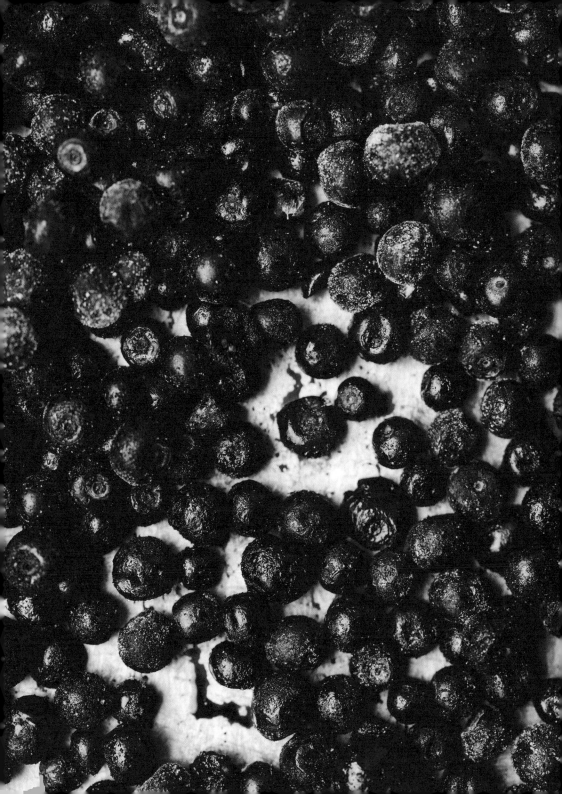

KIWI, KALE & CHIA PARFAIT

SERVES 2

Although it doesn't say so on our book cover or blog title, one goal we have had since we started is to make greens sexier. We want to get more people to eat vegetables by showing how beautiful-looking and wonderful-tasting they are. We think this smoothie does just that. Packed with kale and avocado, it still tastes very sweet and fruity and looks rather stunning with its different layers. This can easily be the dessert of a fancy dinner or served as breakfast on a grey Tuesday morning – that's how versatile and, in fact, simple it is!

FOR THE CHIA PUDDING
250 ml (8½ fl oz/1 cup) Coconut Chia Pudding (made with white chai seeds and coconut drinking milk or tinned coconut milk) (page 28)

FOR THE KIWI FRUIT SMOOTHIE
¼ ripe avocado, stone removed
1 ripe green kiwi fruit
1 frozen banana (page 22)
1 handful kale or spinach, stems removed (organic if possible)
125 ml (4 fl oz/½ cup) coconut water (or coconut milk)
juice of ½ lime

TO SERVE
ripe green kiwi fruit, finely sliced and chopped
Nut Butter (page 26)
fresh blueberries
Coconut & Buckwheat Granola (page 29), or granola of choice
desiccated coconut
fresh lemon balm leaves, optional

Add the avocado and kiwi fruit flesh to a blender along with the rest of the kiwi fruit smoothie ingredients.

continued overleaf

Blend on a high speed until completely smooth.

Spoon half of the chia pudding into the base of two medium-sized glasses (as featured in the photo on page 98). For a beautiful artistic look, you don't need to worry about making the layers even.

Arrange a few kiwi fruit slices around the inside of the glasses. Cover with half of the kiwi fruit smoothie, the rest of the chia pudding and a dollop of nut butter. Top with the rest of the kiwi fruit smoothie and finish with another dollop of nut butter, as well as some chopped kiwi fruit and blueberries and a sprinkling of granola, coconut and lemon balm.

KEFIR BIRCHER WITH MIDDLE-EASTERN CITRUS SALAD

If you are already familiar with the concept of overnight oats and Bircher, you know what a creamy and soothing breakfast it is. But then you also know that its pale and somewhat sad-looking appearance often scares away non-believers. This is the ultimate solution. Our tummy-loving Bircher uses a kefir smoothie as a base, which adds healthy, live bacteria that are great for your gut. It is topped with the most beautifully bright and juicy citrus salad, with golden raisins, chopped pistachios and bee pollen. A real stunner in both appearance and flavour!

FOR THE TUMMY-LOVING KEFIR BIRCHER
375 ml (13 fl oz/1½ cups) kefir (cultured milk with live and active bacteria)
1 ripe banana, peeled
1 teaspoon fresh ginger, grated (or ½ teaspoon ground ginger)
1–2 teaspoons quality raw honey
1 teaspoon bee pollen
90 g (3¼ oz/1 cup) rolled oats (choose certified gluten-free if allergic)
1 tablespoon golden linseeds
FOR THE CITRUS SALAD
1 pink or regular grapefruit
1 regular or blood orange
1 clementine or tangerine
TO SERVE
golden raisins or brown raisins (organic if possible)
pistachio nuts, finely chopped
bee pollen
fresh mint leaves, finely sliced
quality raw runny honey
kefir

continued overleaf

Put the kefir, banana, ginger, honey and bee pollen in a blender and blend on a high speed until completely smooth. Taste and adjust the sweetness to your liking by adding more honey if necessary. Pour into a bowl, stir in the oats and linseeds and set aside to soak in the fridge for at least an hour or overnight.

When ready to serve, using a sharp knife, remove the peel and white pith from the citrus fruits and cut along either side of the white membrane to remove the segments.

Spoon the Bircher into two medium-sized bowls (one of which is featured in the photo), top with the citrus segments and finish with a sprinkling of golden raisins, pistachios, bee pollen and mint as well as a drizzle of honey and a dash of kefir on the side.

NUT MILKS
—

'Vrooom, vroooom,' our son says every time he sees us filling the blender with ingredients. There are a million things in this world that he doesn't understand yet, but the blender is *not* one of them. He just learned how to walk, but can already pull a chair to the kitchen counter and drag himself up on it so that he can reach the switch to turn on the blender. He then loves to watch with his big blue eyes as the blender transforms fruit and vegetables into smoothies or pulverizes nuts into nut milks. It is a kind of magic, I must agree, how something as hard as nuts and seeds can be turned in a few seconds into something rich and creamy like almond, sesame or cashew milk. And Isac must feel like a little wizard as he balances on that chair, flipping the switch (with our supervision), turning solids into liquids.

Whether you are vegan, dairy intolerant/allergic or just looking for a change from cow's milk, you will find a good selection of plant milks in this chapter, both natural and flavoured. If you are worrying about calcium deficiency, nature's best calcium sources are dark leafy greens, sesame seeds, almonds and figs, which you get plenty of when you follow the recipes in this book.

BASIC NUT MILK

MAKES 1 LITRE
1¾ pints/4 cups
—

This is our standard recipe for nut and seed milk. We always start with these proportions and, depending on which nuts or seeds we are using, add sweetener to some and spices to others. For a thinner, subtler and more affordable milk, try adding an extra cup of filtered water.

—

150 g (5 oz/1 cup) raw nuts of choice (or a combination of nuts and seeds) (plus filtered water for soaking*)

2–4 soft dried dates, pitted (optional)

¼ teaspoon vanilla powder or 1 teaspoon vanilla extract (optional)

1 litre (1¾ pints/4 cups) filtered water

¼ teaspoon sea salt

—

* *To reduce the phytic acid levels in nuts and seeds, soaking is important. All grains, nuts and seeds contain varying quantities of phytic acid, which affects the mineral absorption in the body. Small amounts of phytic acid aren't unhealthy, but reducing your overall intake is important as it will help you absorb the minerals from the food you're eating.*

Place the nuts in a bowl, cover with filtered water and soak for 8–12 hours in the morning or overnight.

Drain and rinse the nuts, discarding the soaking water. Add them to a blender along with the rest of the ingredients.

** *Be thrifty and save the nut pulp to make our delicious Nut Pulp Crackers (pages 46–47).*

Blend on a high speed until completely smooth. Taste and adjust the sweetness to your liking by adding more dates if necessary (if using).

Strain the nut milk through a nut milk bag, piece of cheesecloth or a fine-mesh sieve** and store in the fridge in a large glass carafe with a lid/stopper. It can keep for a few days in the fridge, if sealed.

—

TIP: *A nut milk bag is a little bag that filters pulp from nut milks, making them entirely smooth and creamy. Nut milk bags can be found in larger kitchen stores or online. You can also replace them with a thin cloth over a fine-mesh sieve.*

STRAWBERRY CASHEW MILK

MAKES 1 LITRE
1¾ pints/4 cups
—

This lush and creamy strawberry 'milkshake' is made from soaked cashew nuts. We add dates as a natural sweetener, but the real flavour comes from the strawberries. Depending on how ripe and sweet your strawberries are, you might like to deduct or add a date or two. When served in small bottles, this milk is ideal for a kids' birthday party. It would also be delicious served with a bowl of porridge or muesli.

150 g (5 oz/1 cup) raw cashew nuts (plus filtered water for soaking)
750 ml (25 fl oz/3 cups) filtered water
225 g (8 oz/1½ cups) fresh ripe strawberries, tops removed (or frozen, thawed) (organic if possible)
4–6 soft dates, pitted
¼ teaspoon ground cardamom
1–2 pinches sea salt
2–3 ice cubes

Place the cashews in a bowl, cover with filtered water and soak for 3–12 hours in the morning or overnight.

Drain and rinse the cashews, discarding the soaking water. Add them to a blender along with the water and blend on a high speed until very smooth. For a creamy velvet texture, leave as is. Alternatively, for a silky smooth texture, strain the cashew milk through a nut milk bag (see tip on page 106), piece of cheesecloth or a fine-mesh sieve. Rinse out the blender and then return the cashew milk to the blender.

Add the rest of the ingredients to the blender and blend on a high speed until completely smooth. Taste and adjust the sweetness to your liking by adding more dates if necessary.

TIP: *For a thinner, subtler and more affordable milk, try adding an extra cup of filtered water.*

Store in the fridge in a large glass carafe with a lid/stopper. It can keep for a few days in the fridge, if sealed.

When ready to serve, pour into medium-sized glass bottles and serve with straws.

SESAME SEED MILK

MAKES 1 LITRE
1¾ pints/4 cups

—

NUT-FREE

Sesame seeds are a great source of calcium; in fact, we often add a couple of tablespoons of tahini (sesame seed paste) to our regular smoothies for a quick calcium boost. By soaking sesame seeds and blending them into a milk or cream, they are even easier for the body to absorb. Another advantage of this milk is that it's entirely nut-free. Sesame seed milk is an acquired taste, as even hulled sesame seeds still have a bitter undertone. To balance the bitterness, we often add a couple of dates, but feel free to add some more if you wish. Alternatively, make the Orange Sesame Smoothie with Muddled Raspberries (page 81), before moving on to this more intense pure sesame seed milk.

—

* For a more nutritious milk, try replacing half of the hulled sesame seeds with unhulled ones.

—

TIP: *To make the Sesame Seed Cream featured in the Orange Sesame Smoothie with Muddled Raspberries, use this recipe but add just 500 ml (17 fl oz/2 cups) filtered water.*

150 g (5 oz/1 cup) raw hulled sesame seeds* (plus filtered water for soaking)

2–4 soft dates, pitted

¼ teaspoon vanilla powder or 1 teaspoon vanilla extract

1 litre (1¾ pints/4 cups) filtered water

¼ teaspoon sea salt

Place the sesame seeds in a bowl, cover with filtered water and soak for 8 hours in the morning or overnight.

Drain and rinse the sesame seeds, discarding the soaking water. Add them to a blender along with the rest of the ingredients. Blend on a high speed until completely smooth. Taste and adjust the sweetness to your liking by adding more dates if necessary.

Strain the sesame seed milk through a nut milk bag (see tip on page 106), piece of cheesecloth or a fine-mesh sieve and store in the fridge in a large glass carafe with a lid/stopper. The milk can keep for a few days in the fridge, if sealed.

ICED ALMOND CHAI LATTE

MAKES 1 LITRE
1¾ pints/4 cups
—

Chilled chai is an interesting taste sensation as the spices have very warm flavours. This is our shortcut to chai, where we simply cut open quality chai tea bags and mix them with almond milk, instead of gathering all the spices and herbs and boiling them together. This chai milk is just as delicious warm too – just gently heat the milk in a pot.

—

* Choose a quality tea brand that uses real chai spices in their products. Our favourites are Pukka, Clipper or Yogi, but there are many great local brands out there as well.

150 g (5 oz/1 cup) raw almonds (plus filtered water for soaking)
3 sachets quality chai tea*, cut open (approx. 6 g/¼ oz)
2–4 soft dried dates, pitted
1 litre (1¾ pints/4 cups) filtered water
¼ teaspoon sea salt
TO SERVE
ice cubes

Place the almonds in a bowl, cover with filtered water and soak for 8–12 hours overnight.

Drain and rinse the almonds, discarding the soaking water. Add them to a blender along with the rest of the ingredients.

Blend on a high speed until completely smooth. Taste and adjust the sweetness to your liking by adding more dates if necessary.

Strain the chai milk through a nut milk bag (see tip on page 106), piece of cheesecloth or a fine-mesh sieve and store in the fridge in a large glass carafe with a lid/stopper.

The chai latte can keep for a few days in the fridge, if sealed. When ready to serve, pour into medium-sized glasses filled with the ice cubes.

TURMERIC TONIC

Turmeric and ginger have been used within Ayurvedic medicine and cooking for thousands of years and warm turmeric milk, 'haldi ka doodh', is still a popular home remedy in India. Apart from its health benefits, it makes a very soothing drink with a touch of sweetness from honey and a kick from turmeric and ginger. We have been making varieties of this for years and it's good served both warm and cold. Be advised, though, turmeric is an acquired taste so start with a little less if you are not used to its flavour. Be sure to add the black pepper – it increases the bioavailability of curcumin, the active component of turmeric.

—

150 g (5 oz/1 cup) mixed raw almonds and cashews (plus filtered water for soaking)
4 teaspoons fresh turmeric, grated (or 2 teaspoons ground turmeric)
2–4 teaspoons fresh ginger, grated (or 1–2 teaspoons ground ginger)
1–2 tablespoons quality raw honey (manuka if possible)
2 teaspoons rosehip powder (optional)
¼ teaspoon vanilla powder or 1 teaspoon vanilla extract
1 litre (1¾ pints/4 cups) filtered water
¼ teaspoon sea salt
pinch black pepper

—

Place the nuts in a bowl, cover with filtered water and soak for 8–12 hours in the morning or overnight.

Drain and rinse the nuts, discarding the soaking water. Add them to a blender along with the rest of the ingredients.

Blend on a high speed until completely smooth. Taste and adjust the spiciness and sweetness to your liking by adding more ginger and/or honey, if necessary.

Strain the turmeric milk through a nut milk bag (see tip on page 106), a piece of cheesecloth or a fine-mesh sieve and store in the fridge in a large glass carafe with a lid/stopper (as featured in the photo*). The tonic can keep for a few days in the fridge, if sealed.

When ready to serve, pour into medium-sized glasses. Alternatively, pour the milk into a saucepan, bring to a gentle simmer, remove from the heat and store in a thermos to take on a picnic.

CHOCOLATE MILK

MAKES 1 LITRE
1¾ pints/4 cups
—

Every Friday is forest hike day at our daughter's preschool. The kids revel in making huts out of branches, climbing on fallen trees and picking fresh flowers and berries. They all bring along their own packed lunches to enjoy outside in the fresh air. As our Scandinavian winters can be quite harsh, we like to add a thermos full of this hot chocolate milk to our daughter's lunch box, which always goes down a treat! Although we tend to drink this chocolate milk warm, it's just as delicious served chilled and tastes just like store-bought chocolate milk. Or, actually, it tastes better!

—

* *We like to use equal amounts of almonds, cashew nuts and unhulled sesame seeds, but a combination of hazelnuts, cashew nuts and macadamia nuts works well too.*

—

TIP: *If you have a nut allergy, simply use a combination of seeds (equal amounts of sesame seeds and hemp seeds work well) or an oat, rice, soy or coconut drinking milk.*

—

150 g (5 oz/1 cup) raw nuts of choice (or a combination of nuts and seeds)* (plus filtered water for soaking)

1 litre (1¾ pints/4 cups) filtered water

4–6 soft dates, pitted

2 tablespoons cacao powder

¼ teaspoon sea salt

1 teaspoon maca, mesquite or lucuma powder (optional)

—

Place the nuts in a bowl, cover with filtered water and soak for 8–12 hours in the morning or overnight.

Drain and rinse the nuts, discarding the soaking water. Add them to a blender along with the water and blend on a high speed until very smooth.

Strain the nut milk through a nut milk bag (see tip on page 106), piece of cheesecloth or a fine-mesh sieve and rinse out the blender.

Return the nut milk to the blender along with the rest of the ingredients and blend on a high speed until completely smooth. Taste and adjust the sweetness to your liking by adding more dates if necessary.

Store in the fridge in a large glass carafe with a lid/stopper. It can keep for a few days in the fridge, if sealed. When ready to serve, heat and pour into medium-sized glasses or a thermos (as featured in the photo).

NUT PULP CRACKERS

When testing the nut milk recipes for this book, we were left with copious amounts of nut pulp. Hating seeing perfectly good food go to waste, we started doing this delicious cracker recipe to take care of the nut milk by-product. These crackers are so simple and quick to make, are packed with flavour and have a crunchy bite. They are the perfect savoury snack topped with hummus, baba ghanoush, pesto, tapenade, chutney or cheese.

100 g (3½ oz/1 cup) wet nut pulp (from one of our nut milk recipes – see the Nut Milks chapter, page 104)
2 tablespoons linseeds or sesame seeds
¼ small red onion, half finely chopped, half finely sliced
1 teaspoon fresh rosemary and/or thyme, finely chopped
3 tablespoons extra virgin olive oil
½ teaspoon sea salt
½ teaspoon nigella seeds or Za'atar (optional)

Preheat the oven to 160°C/325°F/Gas mark 3 and line a baking tray with parchment paper.

Put the nut pulp, linseeds, sliced onion, half the herbs, oil and salt in a bowl and mix until well combined.

Transfer to the baking tray and shape into a rectangle. Place another piece of parchment paper on top and using a rolling pin, roll into a thin rectangle about 25 cm long × 15 cm wide × 0.3 cm thick (10 in × 6 in × ⅛ inch).

Remove the parchment paper and scatter over the chopped onion and the remaining herbs*. Place the paper back on top and roll a couple more times to press the onion and herbs in place.

*For a Middle Eastern flavour, try adding a sprinkling of nigella seeds and za'atar.

Pierce the crackers lightly with a fork so that they cook evenly. Bake for 10 minutes, then remove from the oven and cut into 5 cm (2 in) squares. Return to the oven for another 20–30 minutes or until golden and crispy.

Cool on a wire rack and serve with your favourite dip or cheese. They can keep for a few days if stored in an airtight container.

JUICES

My grandma always kept a bottle of carrot juice in the fridge. As a kid, I remember tasting it once and immediately spitting it back into the glass, thinking it was the most disgusting drink I had ever tasted. Luise and I got our first juicer twenty years later. Until then, I had stayed far away from all types of carrot juices, and in the beginning, I just focussed on making fruit juices (with heaps of ginger) with our juicer. When Luise finally convinced me to try mixing carrots with oranges (and after that using purely carrots), I couldn't believe how good it was. A completely different flavour from the pasteurized bottle my grandma used to buy.

I can't emphasize enough how much the flavour differs between freshly pressed juice and store-bought pasteurized juice. Not to mention how much healthier it is when all the vitamins and enzymes are still intact.

Nowadays, we have a much higher vegetable-to-fruit ratio in our juices. Some drinks in this chapter are even made purely with vegetables: Cleansing Chlorophyll (page 122), Deeply Rooted (page 127) and Virgin Mary (page 124) are all worth trying!

Flip back to the Tools & Equipment section (page 18) if you want to read our thoughts on which juicer to choose.

DAVID

THREE GREEN JUICES

What I really love about green juices is how fresh they are. I can't understand how orange juice, apple juice and other purely fruit juices have reached such popularity, when, in fact, most juices taste so much better balanced with some greens or vegetables. I realize that it might seem exaggerated to squeeze three sorts of green juices in one small chapter, but they are all very different in flavour and we just couldn't rule any out. One is fresh and sharp, one is entirely vegetable-based and thus not sweet at all, and one has a delicious tropical sweetness to it.
LUISE

SWEET KALE

SERVES 1

—

NUT-FREE

This kale-packed juice has a touch of sweetness from the apples and a fresh punch from the fennel, ginger and lemon. It is a juice recipe that has been on rotation for years in our home and it's still going strong.

---

60 g (2 oz/2 cups) kale, stems removed (organic if possible)
2 small apples, cored (approx. 200 g/7 oz) (organic if possible)
½ small fennel bulb, trimmed (approx. 60 g/2 oz)
½ small lemon, peeled and pips removed (approx. 30 g/1 oz)
1 knob fresh ginger, peeled (approx. 15 g/½ oz)

Wash all of the ingredients and chop them to fit your juicer.

Feed all of the ingredients through the mouth of the juicer one by one, alternating between the fibrous (kale, ginger) and juicy (lemon) ingredients, while using the hard ingredients (apples, fennel) to push everything else through.

Left: Cleansing Chlorophyll; *top right:* Sweet Kale; *bottom right:* Pineapple Greens

continued overleaf

Taste and adjust the flavours to your liking.

Stir well, pour into a medium-sized glass and serve cold or store in a medium-sized sealable glass jar or airtight glass bottle (as featured in the photo) to take on the go.

CLEANSING CHLOROPHYLL

SERVES 1
—
NUT-FREE

I really had to fight to get this one in the book. David always likes to add some kind of fruit when we make green juices, whereas I really appreciate the earthy and grassy flavours of a pure vegetable juice. Since I fought so hard, I do hope you try it! It's a refreshing break from our sweeter recipes, which we all need every now and then.
LUISE

60 g (2 oz/2 cups) spinach, stems included (organic if possible)
20 cm (8 in) piece cucumber (approx. 250 g/9 oz) (organic if possible)
1 celery stalk, with leaves (approx. 50 g/2 oz) (organic if possible)
1 leaf chard, stem included (approx. 30 g/1 oz)
1 handful fresh parsley, stems included (approx. 15 g/½ oz)

Wash all of the ingredients and chop them to fit your juicer.

Feed all of the ingredients through the mouth of the juicer one by one, using the hard ingredients (cucumber, celery) to push the fibrous ingredients (spinach, chard, parsley) through.

Taste and adjust the flavours to your liking.

Stir well, pour into a medium-sized glass and serve cold or store in a medium-sized sealable glass jar or airtight glass bottle (as featured in the photo) to take on the go.

PINEAPPLE GREENS

This is the juice version of our Greens for All smoothie (page 142). Of all the fruits, I believe that pineapple is the perfect match for green vegetables and, when juiced, its flavours are even sweeter and more intense. The addition of fresh mint leaves makes this the most refreshing and tropical green juice we've ever tried.

250 g (9 oz/1½ cups) ripe pineapple, peeled
60 g (2 oz/2 cups) spinach, stems included (organic if possible)
60 g (2 oz/2 cups) lettuce
½ lime, peeled and pips removed (approx. 30 g/1 oz)
10 fresh mint leaves

Wash all of the ingredients and chop them to fit your juicer.

Feed all of the ingredients through the mouth of the juicer one by one, alternating between the fibrous (spinach, lettuce, mint) and juicy (lime) ingredients, whilst using the hard ingredient (pineapple) to push everything else through.

Taste and adjust the flavours to your liking.

Stir well, pour into a medium-sized glass and serve cold or store in a medium-sized sealable glass jar or airtight glass bottle (as featured in the photo) to take on the go.

VIRGIN MARY
HANGOVER CURE

SERVES 2

—

NUT-FREE

We have close friends in London who always take us out for brunch at the weekend whenever we visit. When eating out, they often order Bloody Marys, while at home they make the most delicious fresh juices. So this is my perfect drink for them (and anyone else of course). A non-alcoholic juice version of the Bloody Mary, this Virgin Mary features all the usual suspects, plus a few healthy added extras, including a kick of fresh ginger. We serve it in a sexy salt-rimmed glass filled with ice cubes and topped with freshly ground black pepper and oregano sprigs.

3 plum tomatoes or 24 cherry tomatoes (approx. 300 g/10½ oz) (organic if possible)

1 celery stalk with leaves (approx. 50 g/2 oz) (organic if possible)

½ red (bell) pepper, core and seeds removed (approx. 90 g/3¼ oz) (organic if possible)

1 knob fresh ginger, peeled (approx. 15 g /½ oz)

2 sprigs fresh oregano

1 teaspoon organic unfiltered apple cider vinegar

3 drops Tabasco sauce

2 pinches sea salt

TO SERVE

lime juice

coarse sea salt

ice cubes

freshly ground black pepper

fresh oregano sprigs

Wash the tomatoes, celery, pepper, ginger and oregano and chop them to fit your juicer. Feed them through the mouth of the juicer

continued overleaf

one by one, alternating between the fibrous (oregano, ginger) and juicy (tomatoes, pepper) ingredients, while using the hard ingredient (celery) to push everything else through.

Stir in the apple cider vinegar, Tabasco and salt. Taste and adjust the flavours to your liking.

Stir well, pour into two medium-sized glasses rimmed with lime juice and salt* and filled with ice cubes (one of which is featured in the photo). Finish with a sprinkling of black pepper and a sprig of oregano and serve.

—

* To rim your glasses, on a saucer create a circle of salt bigger in diameter than the rims of your glasses. Moisten the rims of the glasses with lime juice and turn them upside down to dip in the salt.

DEEPLY ROOTED

SERVES 1
—
NUT-FREE

Jam-packed with earthy flavours from four different root vegetables, this juice is also naturally very sweet and refreshing. Beetroot is known to cleanse the liver and purify the blood. Don't go throwing the pulp away, you can, for example, add it to hummus and falafel.

¼ small raw sweet potato, peeled (approx. 75 g/2½ oz)
1 large raw beetroot, peeled (approx. 200 g/7 oz)
2 raw carrots, tops removed and peeled (approx. 200 g/7 oz)
½ small lemon, peeled and pips removed (approx. 30 g/1 oz)
1 knob fresh ginger, peeled (approx. 15 g /½ oz)

Wash all of the ingredients and chop them to fit your juicer.

Feed them through the mouth of the juicer one by one, alternating between the fibrous (ginger) and juicy (lemon) ingredients, while using the hard ingredients (sweet potato, beetroot, carrots) to push everything else through.

Taste and adjust the flavours to your liking.

Stir well, pour into a medium-sized glass and serve cold, or store in a medium-sized airtight glass bottle (as featured in the photo overleaf) to take on the go.

ANTI-INFLAMMATORY MORNING GLORY

SERVES 1

—

NUT-FREE

We often make this juice in the morning when we are starting to feel a little under the weather. It's super-refreshing, almost fiercely so, with a real punch from grapefruit and ginger. Think of it as a superman version of your morning OJ. If you don't wake up after a glass of this, you were probably not meant to get out of bed at all this morning.

2 raw carrots, tops removed and peeled (approx. 200 g/7 oz)
1 grapefruit, peeled and pips removed (approx. 150 g/5 oz)
1 orange, peeled (approx. 150 g/5 oz)
¼ yellow or red (bell) pepper (45 g/1½ oz) (organic if possible)
1 knob fresh ginger, peeled (approx. 15 g /½ oz)
1 knob fresh turmeric, peeled (approx. 7 g /¼ oz) or ¼ teaspoon ground turmeric (to add after juicing)
pinch black pepper

Wash all of the ingredients and chop them to fit your juicer.

Feed them through the mouth of the juicer one by one, alternating between the fibrous (ginger, turmeric) and juicy (grapefruit, orange, pepper) ingredients, while using the hard ingredient (carrots) to push everything else through. Stir in the black pepper.

Taste and adjust the flavours to your liking.

Stir well, pour into a medium-sized glass and serve cold, or store in a medium-sized airtight glass bottle (as featured in the photo) to take on the go.

Left: Anti-Inflammatory Morning Glory; *right:* Deepy Rooted

SPICY APPLE & CARROT 'HOT TODDY'

SERVES 2

NUT-FREE

With our long Scandinavian winters, we wanted to include at least one warm juice. This sweet and spice-infused apple and carrot 'hot toddy' is a perfect nightcap, a soothing cold and flu remedy or simply a comforting treat on a miserable cold and wet day.

4 small apples, cored (approx. 400 g/14 oz) (organic if possible)
2 large carrots, tops removed and peeled (approx. 300 g/10½ oz)
1 knob fresh ginger, peeled (approx. 15 g/½ oz)
¼ teaspoon ground cinnamon
¼ teaspoon ground nutmeg
pinch ground cardamom
pinch ground cloves
TO SERVE
ground cinnamon

Wash the apples, carrots and ginger and chop them to fit your juicer.

Feed them through the mouth of the juicer one by one, alternating between the fibrous (ginger) and juicy (apples) ingredients, while using the hard ingredient (carrots) to push everything else through.

Taste and adjust the flavours to your liking.

Pour the juice into a saucepan and mix in the spices. Bring to a gentle simmer and remove from the heat.

Stir well, pour into two medium-sized mugs (as featured in the photo), finish with a sprinkling of cinnamon and serve straight away.

TIP: *For a winter punch, try adding a dash of rum to the finished 'hot toddy' (1 part rum to 4 parts juice).*

DESSERTS

'I'll be back soon!' David says as he disappears into the kitchen. Both the kids are already tucked up in bed. I can hear some chopping going on, the door to the freezer quietly opening and closing, then, of course, the SLAM of a knife hitting the floor (he always drops something when he tries to be quiet!) – silence … they are still sleeping … a slight whizz from the food processor on minimum speed. A minute later, the sound of dark chocolate being grated and then he shows up with tonight's treat – a strawberry nice cream smoothie topped with fruit, nut butter and lots of dark chocolate!

I'm not sure when it started, but we have become hooked on this evening ritual of making small improvised desserts that we eat while watching TV, reading a book, writing a blog post or answering emails. Sometimes the dessert can simply be stuffed dates or apple slices dipped in nut butter, but most commonly we do various sorts of sweeter smoothies. I love the Triple Chocolate Mint Bowl (page 143), and when apples are in season, David never misses a chance to make his Apple Pie in a Glass (page 135). Even if we have given the smoothies in this chapter a dessert label, you can go right ahead and make them for breakfast if you prefer. We are not going to tell anyone.

LUISE

APPLE PIE
IN A GLASS

SERVES 2

—

NUT-FREE

From the look of this scrumptious three-layered smoothie, it can seem rather daunting to make, when in actual fact it's a bare 15-minute job and the perfect breakfast or dessert solution. It's honestly one of the most delicious little treats we've come up with so far! We sauté aromatic apple pieces in butter, then coat them in a creamy vanilla yoghurt smoothie, followed by a sprinkling of crunchy spiced granola – it's heavenly. Just like the real thing (but healthier).

* You can make the granola topping out of most grains, pseudocereals, seeds and nuts – let your imagination run wild!

FOR THE SPICED GRANOLA*
1 tablespoon butter or cold-pressed coconut oil
1 tablespoon pure maple syrup
½ teaspoon ground cinnamon
¼ teaspoon ground nutmeg
¼ teaspoon ground cardamom
¼ teaspoon ground ginger
4 tablespoons rolled oats (choose certified gluten-free if allergic)
4 tablespoons raw sunflower seeds

FOR THE SAUTÉED APPLE PIECES
1 tablespoon butter or cold-pressed coconut oil
1 cooking apple, peeled and cored (organic if possible)
½ teaspoon ground cinnamon
¼ teaspoon ground ginger

FOR THE VANILLA YOGHURT SMOOTHIE
1 eating apple, cored (organic if possible)
375 g (13 oz/1½ cups) full-fat plain unsweetened Greek yoghurt
½ teaspoon ground vanilla or vanilla extract

continued overleaf

To make the spiced granola, melt the butter and maple syrup in a frying pan (skillet) on a medium heat. Add the spices, shortly followed by the oats and seeds. Stir to coat in the butter mixture and toast for about 5 minutes or until golden. Set aside to cool slightly while you prepare the sautéed apple pieces.

Without rinsing the pan, melt the butter on a medium heat while you cut the apple into 1 cm (½ in) dice. Add the spices, shortly followed by the apple pieces, and sauté for about 5 minutes or until golden, tender and fragrant. Keep warm while you prepare the vanilla yoghurt smoothie.

Roughly chop the apple, add it to a blender along with the rest of the vanilla yoghurt smoothie ingredients and blend on a high speed until completely smooth.

To assemble, divide the apple pieces between two medium-sized glass jars. Pour the yoghurt smoothie on top, finish with a generous sprinkling of the granola and serve. Enjoy!

BOUNTY JARS

SERVES 2
or 4 small servings

—

NUT-FREE

Coconut lovers unite! We present the Bounty Jars of your dreams. You can't go wrong with this healthy interpretation of a classic chocolate bar – a super-tasty and sweet coconut and banana smoothie is layered with a simple silky smooth dark chocolate sauce that makes it look spectacular. It can be prepared in no time and is a real showstopper. We tend to serve this type of smoothie as a dessert, but we are not going to stop you from indulging in it for breakfast!

FOR THE DARK CHOCOLATE SAUCE
4 tablespoons cold-pressed coconut oil
2 tablespoons pure maple syrup
4 tablespoons cacao powder
FOR THE COCONUT & BANANA SMOOTHIE
1 frozen banana (page 22)
50 g (2 oz/½ cup) desiccated coconut
250 ml (8½ fl oz/1 cup) full-fat coconut milk
pinch vanilla powder or extract
2 ice cubes
TO SERVE
toasted coconut chips

Melt the coconut oil and maple syrup in a saucepan on a low heat. Stir through the cacao powder and mix until well combined and silky smooth. Set aside to cool slightly while you prepare the coconut and banana smoothie.

Put all of the coconut and banana smoothie ingredients in a blender and blend on a high speed until completely smooth.

continued overleaf

To assemble, pour just under half of the chocolate sauce into the base of two medium-sized glass jars (as featured in the photo) or four small ones. Cover with half of the coconut and banana smoothie. Repeat with all but a drizzle of the chocolate sauce and the rest of the coconut and banana smoothie.

Finish with a drizzle of chocolate sauce as well as a sprinkling of coconut and serve straight away, while the chocolate sauce is still molten.

ROSEHIP 'AFFOGATO' WITH CRUMBLED 'AMARETTI'

This is a slight deviation from a smoothie as we don't even use a blender, but it's a drink we used to have growing up, so we just couldn't leave it out. Rosehips are a true Scandinavian superfood with a unique flavour. They are packed with anti-inflammatory and antioxidant compounds and are known to reduce pain and improve movement for arthritis sufferers. Luise's 84-year-old grandpa has been adding a tablespoon to his porridge for decades and he swears by it. In Sweden, rosehip powder is sold in supermarkets and health food stores; however, if you live in another country, you can always find it online. You can drink this cold; in fact, rosehip soup is an excellent base in smoothies. Here, however, we serve it exactly how I remember it from my childhood – hot, poured over a dollop of ice cream (or Greek yoghurt) and topped with crushed biscuits.

FOR THE DATE 'AMARETTI'

4–5 soft dates, pitted
90 g (3¼ oz/¾ cup) ground almonds (or almond flour)
60 ml (2 oz/¼ cup) almond milk

FOR THE ROSEHIP SOUP

40 g (1½ oz/¼ cup) rosehip powder
1 tablespoon arrowroot (or potato starch)
500 ml (17 fl oz/2 cups) water
3 tablespoons pure maple syrup

TO SERVE

vanilla ice cream (ordinary or vegan)

---

continued overleaf

Preheat the oven to 180°C/350°F/Gas mark 4 and line a baking tray with parchment paper. Place all of the ingredients for the date 'amaretti' in a food processor and pulse until mixed. Alternatively, put the dates in a bowl and mash them with a fork until they form a paste. Add the rest of the ingredients and mix until well combined. Taste and adjust the sweetness to your liking by adding more dates if necessary. Transfer to a piping bag and pipe into about 2 cm (¾ in) diameter rounds, like amaretti biscuits (Italian macaroons). Bake for about 10 minutes or until golden. Set aside to cool while you prepare the rosehip soup.

Put the rosehip powder in a saucepan along with the arrowroot and water. Bring to the boil, whisking continuously to prevent lumps from forming. Reduce the heat, whisk in the maple syrup and simmer for about 5 minutes, or until a smooth syrup forms, before removing from the heat. Strain it through a fine-mesh sieve to get it completely smooth.

To assemble, spoon a scoop of vanilla ice cream into the base of two medium-sized glass jars or bowls, or in a large jar (as featured in the photo), and pour over the rosehip soup. Finish with a sprinkling of crumbled 'amaretti' and some extra ice cream on top for the sweet-toothed. Serve straight away before it comes running down the glass jar!

TRIPLE CHOCOLATE MINT BOWL

SERVES 2
or 4 small servings
—

Placing this recipe in the Desserts chapter of the book felt like the right thing to do after we threw those dark chocolate squares on top! But if you take a peek at the ingredients, you'll find that it's actually quite a healthy snack. There's even a whole avocado in it, although completely disguised by the dark chocolate and fresh mint flavours. This one is quite rich so you can keep the portion sizes small. And you can obviously just replace the chocolate granola with any granola that you have at home, for an even quicker recipe.

—

For a healthier option, try adding a couple of tablespoons of cacao nibs to the granola topping (at the same time as the oats and quinoa) as opposed to adding the chocolate squares.

FOR THE CHOCOLATE & QUINOA GRANOLA*

1 tablespoon cold-pressed coconut oil

1 tablespoon pure maple syrup

1 tablespoon cacao powder

30 g (1 oz/¼ cup) rolled oats (choose certified gluten-free if allergic)

15 g (½ oz/¼ cup) puffed quinoa (or raw rinsed quinoa, for a crunchier texture)

30 g (1 oz/¼ cup) whole hazelnuts

FOR THE CHOCOLATE SMOOTHIE

1 ripe avocado, stone removed

2 frozen bananas (page 22)

4 tablespoons cacao powder

2 tablespoons hazelnut butter (or any other Nut Butter, page 26)

250 ml (8½ fl oz/1 cup) soya milk (or almond milk)

2–4 drops peppermint oil or 4–8 fresh peppermint leaves

TO SERVE

quality dark chocolate (at least 70% cocoa) or raw vegan refined sugar-free chocolate squares

whole hazelnuts

—

NOTE: The photo features a double recipe.

continued overleaf

Start by making the granola. Melt the coconut oil and maple syrup in a frying pan (skillet) on a low heat. Stir through the cacao powder and mix until well combined and silky smooth. Add the oats, quinoa and hazelnuts, stir to coat in the oil mixture and toast over a medium heat for about 5 minutes or until golden. Set aside to cool on parchment paper in the fridge (or freezer) while you prepare the chocolate smoothie.

Scoop the flesh out of the avocado and add it to a blender along with the rest of the chocolate smoothie ingredients. Blend on a high speed until completely smooth. Taste and adjust the mint flavour to your liking by adding more peppermint oil or leaves if necessary.

To assemble, pour into two small bowls (three are featured in the photo) or four miniature ones. Finish with a sprinkling of the granola and a few hazelnuts. Top with a chocolate square and serve.

STRAWBERRY NICE CREAM & CHOCOLATE QUINOA BIRCHER

If you're not familiar with frozen banana ice cream yet, it's about time you were! Simply blend frozen bananas (page 22) until smooth and in no time you have a lush, creamy and healthy ice cream from nature, called 'nice cream'. The addition of frozen strawberries and coconut milk makes this nice cream extra fluffy and flavoursome. Here we pair it with a thick chocolate quinoa Bircher that will leave you fuller for longer. Practise your layering skills and you will impress any guest with this dessert. You can, of course, serve either the nice cream or the Bircher on their own if you don't have time to prepare both.

FOR THE CHOCOLATE QUINOA BIRCHER

100 g (3½ oz/½ cup) uncooked white quinoa, rinsed (or 1¼ cups cooked)

250 ml (8½ fl oz/1 cup) filtered water

¼ teaspoon sea salt

2 tablespoons cacao powder

120 g (4 oz/½ cup) coconut yoghurt or Greek yoghurt

1 tablespoon pure maple syrup (use 2 tablespoons if you are serving the Bircher on its own)

FOR THE STRAWBERRY NICE CREAM

200 g (7 oz/1¾ cups) frozen strawberries (organic if possible)

1 frozen banana (page 22)

60 ml (2 fl oz/¼ cup) full-fat coconut milk

TO SERVE

fresh strawberries, thinly sliced and whole (organic if possible)

dark chocolate, finely chopped and grated

---

continued overleaf

Put the uncooked quinoa in a saucepan along with the water and salt. Cover and bring to the boil, then reduce the heat and simmer for about 15–20 minutes or until all of the water is absorbed.

Pour into a bowl and leave to cool completely. Add the rest of the Bircher ingredients, mix until well combined and set aside in the fridge while you prepare the strawberry nice cream.

Put all of the strawberry nice cream ingredients in a blender and blend on a high speed until completely smooth, thick and creamy like soft-serve ice cream. Depending on the strength of your blender, you may need to wait 5–10 minutes for the ingredients to thaw slightly (alternatively, use an immersion blender).

To assemble, spoon one third of the nice cream into the base of two medium-sized glass jars or a large one (as featured in the photo). For a beautiful artistic look, make messy uneven layers. Cover with half of the Bircher and press some of the sliced strawberries against the sides of each glass jar. Repeat with the rest of the nice cream, Bircher and strawberries, finishing with a thick layer of the nice cream. To create a marbled effect, simply run the back of a teaspoon up and down along the inside of the glass. Be careful not to mix too much or the layers will blend into one. Finish with a few whole strawberries, as well as a sprinkling of dark chocolate shavings and pieces, and serve straight away before it comes running down the glass jar!

MARBLED SMOOTHIE POPSICLES

MAKES 10 POPSICLES

Our popsicle version of a smoothie has a beautiful marbled look that can be made in an array of colours. The photo features three different flavour combinations: mango and passion fruit; strawberries and raspberries; and blueberries, but you can adapt this recipe to any fruit of choice – just let your imagination run wild! If you choose a very ripe and sweet fruit, you can use a little less sweetener, or increase it if your fruit is very tart.

* For a vegan alternative, try replacing the yoghurt with full-fat plain unsweetened coconut yoghurt or milk. Alternatively, use 300 g (10½ oz/2 cups) raw cashew nuts, soaked in filtered water for 3–12 hours, then rinsed and drained.

TIP: We found our popsicle moulds on Amazon, but if you don't have any, mini paper cups with popsicle sticks or teaspoons inserted in the middle work well too.

FOR THE BANANA SMOOTHIE

2 ripe bananas, peeled

500 g (17 oz/2 cups) full-fat plain unsweetened Greek yoghurt*

2 tablespoons pure maple syrup or quality raw honey

¼ teaspoon vanilla powder or 1 teaspoon vanilla extract

FOR THE FRUIT SMOOTHIE

150 g (5 oz/1 cup) fresh ripe berries or fruit of choice

2 tablespoons pure maple syrup or quality raw honey

FOR THE EXTRAS

fresh ripe berries or fruit of choice, roughly chopped

Nut Butter (page 26)

toasted nuts, roughly chopped

Coconut & Buckwheat Granola (page 29)

quality dark chocolate (at least 70% cocoa) or raw vegan refined sugar-free chocolate, roughly chopped

Roughly chop the bananas and add them to a blender along with the rest of the banana smoothie ingredients.

Blend on a high speed until completely smooth.

continued overleaf

Set aside about 350 g (12 oz/1½ cups) of the banana smoothie, leaving the rest in the blender. Add all of the fruit smoothie ingredients to the blender and blend until completely smooth.

Carefully fill 10 popsicle moulds with the smoothies, alternating between the banana and fruit one to create a marbled look (you can also use the back of a teaspoon or a knife to help create this ripple effect, see page 146). For an even more spectacular look and interesting texture, try adding some of the extras in the moulds between the different coloured layers.

Cover, insert the popsicle sticks and set in the freezer for at least 4 hours until completely firm or overnight. They can keep in the freezer for days, weeks, months, years... (but secretly you know they won't!).

BERRY SMOOTHIE & SALTED CARAMEL SEMIFREDDO

SERVES 14

We wanted to end the book with a bit of a bang, so this scrumptious, three-layer vegan semifreddo happened. Frozen cakes have become one of our most popular treats for birthdays and celebrations and this is our latest favourite. We love the rich and decadent salted caramel layer that balances between the fresh berry smoothie layer on top and the crunchy chocolate base. You get so many different flavours and textures in one thin (or thick!) slice. And the berries in the centre take it to the next level. Someone said that it's the grown-ups' gourmet version of Neapolitan ice cream, which is a perfect description.

FOR THE BASE LAYER

10–12 soft dried dates, pitted

1 tablespoon cold-pressed coconut oil

150 g (5 oz/1 cup) raw sunflower seeds

2 tablespoons cacao powder

pinch sea salt flakes

FOR THE SALTED CARAMEL LAYER

10–15 soft dried dates, pitted

125 ml (4 fl oz/½ cup) filtered water

80 ml (3 fl oz/⅓ cup) cold-pressed coconut oil

60 g (2 oz/¼ cup) hulled tahini

2–3 pinches sea salt flakes

FOR THE BERRY SMOOTHIE LAYER

2 ripe bananas, peeled and roughly chopped

150 g (5 oz/1 cup) raw cashew nuts (pre-soaked)*

150 g (5 oz/1 cup) ripe blackberries (or frozen, thawed)

150 g (5 oz/1¼ cups) ripe raspberries (or frozen, thawed)

4 tablespoons lemon juice

2–4 tablespoons filtered water

2 tablespoons pure maple syrup

* Place the cashews in a bowl, cover with filtered water and soak for 3–12 hours in the morning or overnight. Drain and rinse the cashews, discarding the soaking water, and set aside.

continued overleaf

5 fresh ripe blackberries (or frozen, thawed)
12 fresh ripe raspberries (or frozen, thawed)
TO SERVE
fresh blackberries
fresh raspberries
edible pansy petals, optional
icing (confectioners) sugar, to dust

———

Line a 10 × 20 cm (4 × 8 in) loaf tin with parchment paper.

To make the base layer, put the dates and oil in a food processor and blend on a high speed until a sticky paste forms. Add the seeds, cacao and salt and blend again until the mixture resembles coarse breadcrumbs and holds together when pinched. You may need to add a few more dates to achieve the right consistency. Transfer to the loaf tin and, using the palm of your hand or the back of a spoon, press the mixture down firmly to create an even and compact base. Set aside in the freezer while you prepare the salted caramel layer.

Put all of the salted caramel layer ingredients into a blender and blend on a high speed until completely smooth. Taste and adjust the sweetness and saltiness to your liking by adding more dates or salt.

Remove the loaf tin from the freezer and pour the salted caramel layer over the base layer. Tap the tin lightly to smooth out the surface. Return to the freezer while you prepare the berry smoothie layer.

Rinse the blender. Add the bananas to the blender along with the rest of the berry smoothie ingredients. Blend on a high speed until smooth. Add extra water, if needed.

Remove the loaf tin from the freezer and create the berry centre by placing the berries in a centred line on top of the caramel layer. Top with the berry smoothie layer and, using a spatula, smooth out the surface. Tap the tin lightly on the worktop to remove any air bubbles.

Set in the freezer for at least 4 hours or overnight until completely firm. When ready to serve, thaw for about 30 minutes and top with fresh berries and edible petals and sprinkle with icing sugar. Use a sharp knife dipped in hot water to cut 1.5 cm (½ in) slices.

ABOUT THE AUTHORS

David Frenkiel and Luise Vindahl are the couple behind the award-winning vegetarian food blog *Green Kitchen Stories*, which has followers from all over the world. Healthy, seasonal and delicious vegetarian recipes paired with colourful and beautiful photographs have become the trademark of their style. They are also the authors of two internationally acclaimed cookbooks, *The Green Kitchen* and *Green Kitchen Travels*, published by Hardie Grant UK.

David and Luise's work has appeared in *Food & Wine Magazine*, *Bon Appetit*, *ELLE*, *Vogue*, *The Guardian*, *Vegetarian Times* and many more publications. In 2013 and 2015 their blog was winner in the Saveur Magazine Best Food Blog Awards. They have released two best-selling apps for iPhone and iPad, which have been selected in the App Store Best of 2012, 2013 and 2014.

Luise is Danish and David is Swedish. They currently live in Stockholm with their daughter Elsa and son Isac. Apart from doing freelance recipe development and food photography, David works as a freelance graphic designer and Luise is a qualified nutritional therapist.

Read more on www.greenkitchenstories.com

INDEX

Green Kitchen Smoothies by David Frenkiel and Luise Vindahl

First published in 2016 by Hardie Grant Books

Hardie Grant Books (UK)
52–54 Southwark Street
London SE1 1UN
hardiegrant.co.uk

Hardie Grant Books (Australia)
Ground Floor, Building 1
658 Church Street
Melbourne, VIC 3121
hardiegrant.com.au

British Library Cataloguing-in-Publication Data. A catalogue record for this book is available from the British Library.

ISBN: 978-1-78488-046-0

Publisher: Kate Pollard
Senior Editor: Kajal Mistry
Editorial Assistant: Hannah Roberts
Photographer: David Frenkiel
Art Direction and Design: Nicky Barneby
Illustrations: Katrin Coetzer
Recipe tester: Nicola Moores
Copy Editor: Kay Delves
Proofreader: Lorraine Jerram
Indexer: Cathy Heath
Colour Reproduction by p2d

Printed and bound in China by 1010

10 9 8 7 6 5 4 3 2 1

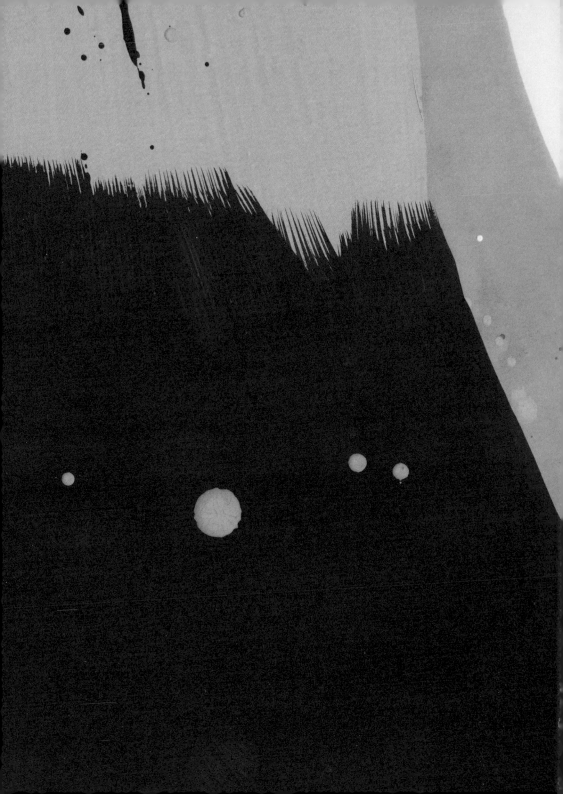